(continued from front flap)

"A manifest gap in African studies has been filled to a very large degree by the work of Professor Filesi . . ." *Race*

". . . it has become the most up-to-date and complete treatment of the subject. There are important pages dedicated to the discovery of Chinese porcelain and coins on the coast of East Africa . . . The work is completed by a very rich bibliography." *East and West*

". . . there are few omissions and the excellent bibliography at the end covers the whole field of Chinese maritime activity up to the end of the Middle Ages. . . . all the evidence from both Chinese documents and East African excavations is considered." *Journal of African History*

CASS LIBRARY OF AFRICAN STUDIES

GENERAL STUDIES
No. 144

Editorial Adviser: JOHN RALPH WILLIS
Department of History, University of California, Berkeley

CHINA AND AFRICA
IN THE
MIDDLE AGES

Some other CENTRAL ASIAN RESEARCH CENTRE Publications

Books, Monographs, Maps, etc.

The USSR and Arabia, by STEPHEN PAGE
Problems of Turkish Power in the Sixteenth Century, by W. E. D. ALLEN
An Introduction to the Turkmen Language, by G. K. DULLING
The Hazaragi Dialect of Afghan Persian, by G. K. DULLING
The Turkish Language of the Soviet Azerbaijan, by C. G. SIMPSON
Some Features of the Morphology of the Oirot (Gorno-Altai) Language, by C. G. SIMPSON
Map of Soviet Central Asia and Kazakhstan, with Introduction, Gazetteer and Glossary
Cities of Central Asia. Town plans, photographs and descriptions of major cities of Soviet Central Asia

Occasional Publications Series

The Mizan Series. Occasional studies on Asian and African topics. No. 1, *Soviet Views on Judaism, Zionism and Israel* (forthcoming, 1972). Later titles will be *Soviet Views on Islam; Soviet Africanists, A Directory and Guide*; and *Soviet Views on African Leaderships*

Periodicals

USSR and the Third World. Issued 10 times p.a. Provides a comprehensive and systematic coverage of reports and comment from all sources on Soviet and Chinese relations with the countries of Asia, Africa and Latin America
Central Asian Review (1953–1968). A quarterly review of Soviet writing on Soviet Central Asia and adjacent countries
Mizan (1959–1971). Articles on Soviet relations with the Middle East, and later (from 1960) Africa, and (from 1966) Asia

Microfilm Publications

Yuva Newsletter (1962–1965: articles and reports on Soviet and Chinese relations with South–East Asia) and *Mizan Supplements* (1966–1970: reports on Soviet and Chinese relations with Asia and Africa)

CENTRAL ASIAN RESEARCH CENTRE
1B Parkfield Street, London N1 OPR

CHINA AND AFRICA
IN THE
MIDDLE AGES

Teobaldo Filesi
Director, Istituto Italiano per l'Africa

Translated by
DAVID L. MORISON
Director, Central Asian Research Centre

Published in Association with the
CENTRAL ASIAN RESEARCH CENTRE

FRANK CASS : LONDON

First published 1972 in Great Britain by
FRANK CASS AND COMPANY LIMITED
67 Great Russell Street, London WC1B 3BT, England

and in United States of America by
FRANK CASS AND COMPANY LIMITED
c/o International Scholarly Book Services, Inc.
P.O. Box 4347, Portland, Oregon 97208

in association with the
CENTRAL ASIAN RESEARCH CENTRE

ISBN 0 7146 2604 X

Printed in Great Britain by
Billing & Sons Ltd, Guildford and London

Contents

List of Illustrations   vii

Preface   ix

I   Introduction   1

II   From the Han Dynasty to the T'ang and Sung Dynasties   4

III   The Expansion and Deployment of China's Navy   12

IV   The Earliest Chinese Descriptions of African Countries   18

V   China's Westward Ventures in the Early Ming Period   26

VI   Chinese Accounts of Brava, Giumbo and Mogadishu   36

VII   Chinese Coins and Porcelain on the East African Coast   41

VIII   The Dates of the Early Ming Voyages to the West   52

IX   Cheng Ho's Two Inscriptions   56

X   The Ending of the Chinese Expeditions to the Western Seas and Africa   66

References   73

Bibliography   90

Index   97

Illustrations

1 Land and sea trade routes between the West and China in the first and second centuries AD   *Page* 6

2 Chinese junk, early nineteenth century
3
4 Various types of ancient Chinese war junks
5
   Between pages 16–17

Facing page

6 Painting of the giraffe sent to the Chinese Court from Bengal   24
7 The inscription found at Ch'ang-lo   25
8 Chinese coins found in coastal areas in Somalia: reverse   40
9 Chinese coins found in coastal areas in Somalia: obverse   41

10 Chinese vase with dragons in grey-blue on a grey ground, mid-fourteenth century, found at Kilepwa
11 Late Ming blue-and-white plate found near the Mosque at Gedi
12 Copper-red vase found in the upper level by the Great Mosque of Gedi
13 Celadon plate found at Gedi
14 Ming blue-and-white porcelain plate found set into a tomb pillar at Mambrui
   Between pages 48–49

15 Section of the Wu-pei-chih map showing the East African coasts visited by Chang Ho   *Page* 57
16 Indian Ocean trade routes in the fifteenth century   58

Preface

With the present study I have endeavoured to reconstruct a chapter in the relations between Asia and Africa in medieval times. Its striking events—and in particular the Chinese naval expeditions to the Western seas and to East Africa in the early Ming period—merit a patient enquiry into their causes and their effects. It is my hope that the present work, offered to the Africanists of my country, may also find acceptance among Africans interested in Africa's contacts with the outside world in pre-colonial times.

I have no pretentions to invade the territory of the Sinologists—and I am extremely grateful to them for the generous assistance they have afforded me. My thanks go, first, to Professor A. F. P. Hulsewé of the Sinologisch Instituut in Leyden; his authoritative and patient guidance has been of crucial value. I owe particular thanks to Dr. Lionello Lanciotti, Librarian of the Istituto per il Medio ed Estremo Oriente in Rome, for the assistance he has given me, and to Professor Joseph Needham of Gonville and Caius College, Cambridge.

To many others, in Africa and Italy, I am sincerely grateful for suggestions and for documentary or other assistance and for unstinting helpfulness on every occasion. Among these I would first thank Professor James Kirkman, Warden of the Coastal Historical Sites of Kenya and a prime authority on Kenya's historical monuments and archaeology, for putting so much interesting and invaluable information at my disposal. I am also much indebted to Professor Neville Chittick; Mr. R. H. Carcasson; Mr. Stanley West; Mr. T. M. Unwin; Mrs. Mary Clifford; the editors of *Tanganyika Notes and Records*; Professor Th. Monod of the Institut Français d'Afrique Noire in Dakar; and Mr. E. J. Brill of Leyden, the editor and publisher of *T'oung Pao*. I am also grateful to my friend Dr. Elio Venzo in Rhodesia for his kindly help, and to my friend Dr. Michele Pirone for his ever-ready assistance from Mogadishu.

I would also offer my thanks to all others in Italy who have so kindly assisted my researches. They include the authorities of the Biblioteca Vaticana, the Biblioteca dell'Accademia dei Lincei and the Biblioteca del Pontificio Istituto Biblico; Dr. Olga Pinto of the Biblioteca Nazionale Vittorio Emanuele II; the Librarian of the British Academy in Rome; my friend Dr. Armano Cepollaro, Librarian of the Istituto Italiano per l'Africa; Professor L. V. Grottanelli; Professor Mordini; and my friend Dr. Antonio Leva, to whom I am indebted for some very useful details.

1962   TEOBALDO FILESI

I

Introduction

The purpose of these notes is to throw light on a striking episode in the relations between the Asian and African continents during what were our own late Middle Ages. Scholarship has done much in recent years to fill the gaps in this chapter of history and to clarify disputed points resulting from the scarcity of first-hand sources. It therefore seems useful to present a conspectus of the available scholarly material, and to include collateral data on finds of Chinese porcelain and coins on the East African coast which date from this period and provide evidence of direct and indirect contacts between China and Africa.[1]

In the view of some writers, modern historical criticism of the documents of the Ming dynasty would tend to indicate that information on African countries collected by the Chinese was obtained not in Africa but in the port of Hormuz or in some other coastal centre on the Persian Gulf, where Chinese, Arab and African traders, merchants and sailors would meet more often and more easily than on the coast of Africa itself. It would thus be a case not of direct contacts and first-hand information, collected by intrepid sailors of the Celestial Empire on Africa's eastern shores, but of second-hand information which, obtained in more accessible parts of the Asiatic continent, has been dressed up as first-hand.[2]

Distinguished Sinologists like Pelliot and Duyvendak consider that this theory can only be sustained in so far as concerns the earlier T'ang and Sung dynasties. Yet, even for these earlier periods, some Chinese sources refer not only to the import of African goods into China but also to visits by Chinese missions and merchants to the African coast in periods preceding the great maritime expeditions undertaken under the first Ming Emperors.[3]

In support of this theory of earlier contacts, some Western scholars cite the evidence of medieval maps and accounts by Arab and European travellers. Schwarz writes: "The most striking testimony of the truth that the Chinese did do a great trade with East Africa is afforded by the maps of the period. There is the Catalan Atlas of 1375, but earlier editions existed; this shows Chinese ships sailing about the Indian Ocean, with meticulous regard to details of construction and rigging. Fra Mauro's map is less correct about the actual design, but it shows the immense junks followed by two smaller ones, acting as store ships, exactly as described by Ibn Battuta in 1340. . . . The trade with East Africa began certainly in the Sung dynasty, 960–1280, if not before; there is mention in the 'Book of the Marvels of India' of a fleet that sailed in 945. . . . Al Biruni was on the Arabian coast and saw the fleets of junks, which he describes in his 'Geography', 1040. Idris, 1154, is equally explicit; he states that the Chinese transferred their trade to the island of Zanj (Zanzibar), which is off the coast of Zinj, and by their equity, mild ways and accommodating spirit, soon came into very intimate relations with the inhabitants. Those 'intimate relations' produced a fine crop of half-caste children up and down the coast. . . . They can still today be recognized by their yellow skins and other Mongoloid characteristics. Mas'udy, in his 'Golden Meadows', says that to the south of the country of the blacks (Zinj) there were the Wa-Kwakwa, who were related to the Chinese, they themselves being known as Gog and Magog . . . Ma-gog is the Bantu plural of Gog."[4]

But these notices of chroniclers or geographers or Arab travellers on which Schwarz and others rely were often, in their turn, based on second-hand sources or fantastic interpretations. They have not yet afforded any irrefutable proof of the effective presence or appearance of the Chinese on the coasts of East Africa before the spectacular expeditions undertaken with the advent of the Ming dynasty.[5]

As regards these expeditions, the painstaking studies of Rockhill, Hirth, Pelliot and Duyvendak during the period between the two world wars have removed any doubt about the factual evidence for the visits to the African coast of the Chinese fleets directed by the grand eunuch Cheng Ho, and have also succeeded in establishing their dates with some precision.[6]

These expeditions, which are the subject of special discussion later in this study, are important as a proof not only of Chinese nautical proficiency in a period when the European seafaring nations had not yet embarked on their great adventures, but also of the scale of the relations already subsisting at that period between continents almost wholly cut off from the influences of the western European world.

In their voyages to and from the Arabian peninsula and the Horn of Africa the Chinese fleets were of course carried, in turn, by the north-east and south-west monsoon winds. The purposes of these visits were those of commerce, and also of prestige. The Chinese were not conquerors in principle. The rulers of the Celestial Empire considered themselves to be invested with a universal authority. This authority needed to be revealed, and to be met with a corresponding act of homage in return; it did not need to be imposed. It was only when this rule was not observed or was transgressed by "barbarian peoples" that the Chinese turned themselves into warriors who would reimpose the order that had been violated.[7]

After the second century AD, with the formation of the states of Java and Sumatra in Indonesia, groups of Malay origin succeeded—using vessels which still today remain an intriguing mystery—in making their final landfall in the island of Madagascar. There they settled and gave birth to the Malagasy civilization, which remains the most concrete and productive expression of the contacts between furthest Asia and the world of Africa. Although the routes followed by these seafarers are still debated, it would appear from some traces they left of their passage that they coasted along the present Somalia, making stops at the numerous small Bajun islands opposite the coast south of the Juba river. Their last expedition must have been in the sixteenth century, when the new arrivals proceeded to the occupation of the eastern part of the Great Island.[8]

II

From the Han Dynasty to the T'ang and Sung Dynasties

The history of China's relations with the coastal peoples of East Africa dates back to times not less remote than those which saw the first migrations of Malaysian peoples to the island of Madagascar.

From the second and third centuries AD—that is, from the time of the great expansion of the Roman Empire towards Africa and the East—there were fairly close contacts both by land and sea between the peoples of East Africa and the Roman–Greek–Egyptian world. So far as concerns Egypt, the province of Roman Africa which lay on these lines of communication, with its great commercial and cultural magnet of Alexandria, these contacts would merit a separate study. Hudson's study of them is notable, with its identification of the trade routes between China and the West from the first and second centuries AD onward (fig. 1).[9]

Pelliot seems to consider it possible that in Han times (from the beginning of the first to the beginning of the third centuries AD) the Chinese reached Egypt by the overland route, and reached a city mentioned in the *Wei-lüeh* or *Wei-lio* (a chronicle of the state of Wei, one of the "Three Kingdoms", composed between AD 239 and 265) under the name of Wu-ch'i-san, corresponding, according to Hirth, to the city of Alexandria.[10]

However, certain information on the maritime trade under the Han dynasty and under the usurper Wang Mang, contained in the *Ch'ien-Han shu*, leads one to conclude that as early as the first century BC the Chinese may have reached quite distant Western countries by the sea route, thanks to an organizing technique which in its main outline was to be resumed fourteen centuries later by the first Ming Emperors.[11] The *Ch'ien-Han shu* not only lists and describes the various foreign countries but also specifies that all offered their tribute, and that there were at the Court Heads of the interpreters, in the service of the Yellow Gate, or the Department of Eunuchs: "Together with volunteers they are sent overseas to acquire pearls, rare stones and exotic products, in exchange for which they offer gold and varied silks. The countries they visit supply them with provisions, and furnish them with escorts for their journeys. The

4

barbarians' merchant ships carry them on until they reach their destination; they [the barbarians] also get profit from the trade, [and sometimes] rob and kill the people. . . . In the *Yüan-shih* period Emperor P'ing (AD 1–6) Wang Mang (the usurper) wished to confer greater lustre on his imperial glory. He sent rich gifts to the King of Huang-chih, and secured from the latter in return the dispatch of an envoy [with the mission] of presenting [as tribute] a live rhinoceros. From Huang-chih, after about eight months' sail, one gets to P'i-tsung; after eight months' sail one gets to the border of Hsiang-lin in Jih-nan [in central Annam]. The Han envoy-interpreter got home from there.'[12]

What remains somewhat obscure in this episode is the provenance of such an animal as the rhinoceros. Some scholars, such as Herrmann and Hennig, identify the country of Huang-chih with Abyssinia. Herrmann, indeed, discovers a certain phonetic resemblance between *Huang-chih* and the *Ag'azi* or *Ge-ez* of the Abyssinian coast. This, as Duyvendak observes, seems far-fetched.[13] Nor can one regard as conclusive the fact that Abyssinian rhinoceroses were particularly renowned. One must consider, on the one hand, the great difficulty in transporting such an animal in those days from such distant parts, and on the other the fact that there were rhinoceroses in regions much nearer to China, as in Indonesia and India. The references contained in the *Ch'ien-Han shu* are, however, "extremely valuable as an indication of the antiquity of China's trade relations with the countries of the Indian Ocean".

Writings of the period of the "Three Kingdoms" speak of four-masted and even seven-masted ships, "with some kind of fore and aft rig being used by the Chinese of Canton and Annam".[14] But it seems more probable that it was only during the period 420–479 that China began to build ships for maritime trade, and that it was in the seventh century that this new activity really came to the fore, to make the Chinese the boldest seamen of the Orient.[15]

According to Arab sources, under the T'ang dynasty various commodities were exported by sea to the Celestial Empire, principally ivory, incense, copper, tortoiseshell, camphor and rhinoceros horn. The Arabs, sailing from the Persian Gulf, crossed the Indian Ocean and, rounding the Malay peninsula, reached Canton where they transacted their business. Canton was at that time called Khanfou (Khanfu), a rendering of the Chinese Kuang-fu or Kuang-chou.[16]

Foreign products were subject to heavy duties, probably justified by the need to show a spectacular benefit to the treasury in order to silence the school of thinking at Court which opposed any dealings with barbarian peoples and hence any form of foreign trading, maritime trade in particular. Arriving at the great port of Canton,

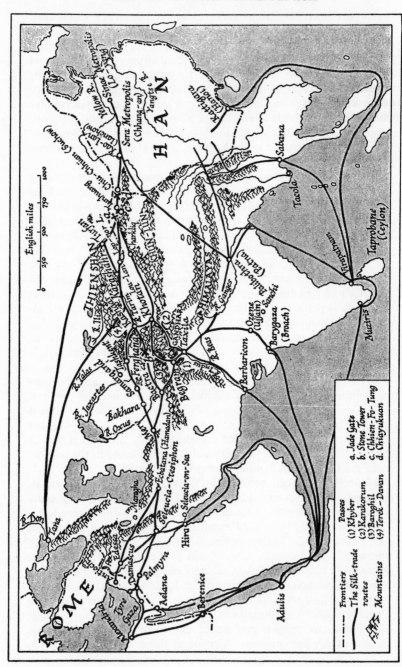

1 Land and sea trade routes between the West and China in the first and second centuries AD *(after Hudson)*

the real heart of the sea trade of the Chinese empire, all the vessels had to surrender their cargoes to the imperial agents, who saw to their warehousing and retention until the conclusion of the sailing season, when the south-west monsoon had carried the last junk home to harbour. They then proceeded to consign seven-tenths of each cargo to its owners, withholding three-tenths for the state by way of import duty. "A truly imperial share in the profits of private enterprise", as Davidson remarks.[17]

The extraordinary expansion of sea trade under the T'ang Emperors (AD 619–906) can be deduced from the *T'ang kuo-shih pu* or "Addenda to the National History of the T'ang", of the ninth century, which, in a kind of retrospective chronicle, speaks of ships of the southern seas which were so high out of the water that ladders some tens of feet long were needed to get aboard them.[18]

However, during this period the Court began to adopt stringent measures to put a stop to the export of coin in large quantities. An edict of the second year of k'ai-yüan (AD 713) laid down that "gold and iron must not be exchanged with any foreigner"; and in the first year of chien-chung (780) another edict ruled that "silver, copper, iron, and slaves male and female must not be traded with any foreigner".[19]

The Court, nevertheless, seems not to have considered the system to be sufficiently watertight: with the advent of the Sung dynasty all the regulations were revised, in 971, in a more rigorous and fiscally more onerous form. Eventually, ten years later, any remaining freedom for private enterprise was removed, maritime commerce with the outside world in any form was declared a monopoly of the state, and the most severe punishments (such as branding on the face and exile to a distant island) were invoked for private persons who traded with foreigners.

This new turn in policy and these drastic measures did not however prevent foreign trade from further development; rather, they made it an instrument of government policy. Although the class of scholar officials regarded with disdain the participation of the state in commercial enterprises, not a few officials and members of the Court acquired direct interests in the shipping and naval construction companies. It is on record that between 984 and 987 the Sung Emperor T'ai-tsung dispatched a mission of eight officials with the aim of encouraging the traders of the southern seas and the Chinese merchants who went overseas to turn towards China.[20]

For the monopolies established by the government in foreign trade and in various productive enterprises the results were eloquent: in the first years of the reign of kao-tsung half the state's revenues derived from the monopoly and percentage taxes, and 20 per cent of the revenues of the treasury coffers came from maritime trade. In an ordinance issued in the seventh year of shao-tsing (1137) the Emperor Kao-tsung himself declared: "The profit derived from foreign trade is most great. When the management was proper the income was sometimes counted by millions (of cash). Is this not far better than taxing the people? It is why we pay much attention to it. We could thus be lenient to the people, and let them be a little more prosperous." And in a later ordinance of the eighteenth year (1146) he declared again: "The profit of marine trade contributes much to the national income. Therefore, pursuing the former custom, the people of far-away countries should be encouraged to come and import an abundant supply of foreign goods."[21]

At the beginning of the Sung dynasty three ports were open to traffic with the outside world, Kuang-chou (Canton), Ming-chou (the present Ning-po) and Hang-chou. These had their offices or inspectorates for merchant shipping, concerned above all to levy duties and to transact all matters connected with foreign trade. The officials in question were known as *San-ssu*, "The Three Officials".[22] During this period the port of Kuang-chou (Canton) practically monopolized the duty revenues, taking more than 90 per cent.

However, with the end of the northern Sung dynasty and the advent of the southern Sung, in the first decades of the twelfth century, the port of Ch'üan-chou in Fukien province made its rapid advance. Forty years after this port was opened the Sung capital was transferred from K'ai-fêng to Hang-chou, with the Court and government, and remained there until the end of the southern Sung period and the Mongol conquest, although the Chinese never dignified the city with the title of capital (*ching-shih*), regarding it only as the temporary residence of the imperial family (*hsing-tsai*).

Foreign trade, encouraged by the government in spite of preoccupations over the ever-growing export of coin, soon led to the port of Ch'üan-chou directly rivalling that of Kuang-chou (Canton); it was finally to surpass it in the first half of the fourteenth century. All vessels sailing to or from China made it their essential point of reference and goal. Marco Polo and Ibn Battuta spoke of it as the greatest trading port in the world.[23]

The Sung Annals relate that between 1049 and 1053 the annual import of ivory, rhinoceros horn, pearls and other products amounted to over 53,000 units of currency, and that in 1115 the annual total rose to 500,000. It was within little more than a century after this date that Chinese porcelain began to reach the western ports of the Indian Ocean in considerable quantities.[24] It was indeed in this period that the manufacture of porcelain attained very notable levels, both in quantity and quality. This was also the period in which the

Zinj empire on the East African coast[25] was at the height of its splendour, its cities and its trade developing prodigiously.

Most of the Chinese coins found on the East African coast, as will be noted below, belong to the T'ang and Sung periods. One can conclude from this that the introduction into commerce of large quantities of valuable porcelain had, especially under the Ming, almost superseded the use of coin, which in any case was prohibited as a means of payment by imperial regulations. Another explanation for the sparse finds of Ming coins may lie in the fact that under this dynasty metal currency was almost entirely replaced by paper.[26]

At all events, the trade evolved principally in the direction of the typical barter transactions, in which Chinese products were exchanged with products of the Arab countries and of Africa, precious objects and rare animals, new accessions perhaps for the Emperor's own zoo in Peking.[27]

The rigid fiscal procedures adopted by China constituted what might be characterized as a protectionist mercantile system. They were based on a strict currency control designed to prevent as far as possible any flight of Chinese currency beyond the confines of the Empire. Above all, this sanction was enforced when, under the Sung dynasty, the expansion of Chinese overseas trade resulted in a real drain on the coinage, which gave serious concern to the imperial administration. An edict obliged Chinese traders to effect payments abroad in barter commodities and not in cash.

In 1147 it was laid down that all Chinese vessels going abroad or foreign ships going home, and all ships going out of the ports of Kuangtung and Fukien, must be inspected to see whether they had cash on board.[28] Punishments for violation were very severe, ranging—according to an early Sung edict (965)—from a year's imprisonment for passing a small sum (two strings of cash) to execution for passing a larger quantity (more than three strings). There was a whole series of informers, who were rewarded when they furnished useful information to the imperial agents. A regulation issued in 1219 specified the commodities to be exhibited in place of cash to pay for foreign products: silks, porcelain, brocades and pottery vessels and objects.

As may be imagined, the shrewdness and the stratagems with which traders in every age and country have managed to evade the most rigorous regulations, when prejudicial to their activities and interests or restrictive of the volume of their business, were not less effective in thirteenth-century China in evading the strict control imposed by the imperial administration. This is proved by a pathetic appeal which in 1219 the ministers addressed to the Celestial Emperor to check "all that quantity of silver and gold which, alas, has been

B

flowing out of the country for trading with distant barbarians!''; and by the proposal (later translated into the above-cited ordinance of the same year) to set up commercial establishments on the borders with foreign countries so as to offer the commodities mentioned in exchange for other products.[29]

The severe restrictions and other measures, however, had in practice the effect of considerably increasing the export of products of the Asiatic Far East, and of limiting but not altogether stopping the flight of Chinese specie towards foreign countries to the south and west of China.[30] Thus, while the exchange of merchandise increased notably (as is shown by the finds of Chinese pottery and porcelain on the Indian Ocean coasts and islands) the discovery of an important quantity of Chinese coins of the Sung period[31] goes to show that money also was not—as indeed it could not be—entirely absent from these commercial dealings.

In any case, the voices of alarm and disapproval at Court were raised not so much against commercial activity *per se* as against the fact that the imports consisted essentially of superfluous luxury goods, and the exports principally of metal coin, as Kuwabara and Duyvendak point out. However, Jung-pang Lo disputes this, emphasizing that "the advantages of the trade were . . . chiefly on the side of the Ming court", and that "as for the strange animals, rare objects and frivolous items, they aroused attention, but they were no more than the bonuses of the trade, not the staple".[32]

The Southern Sung dynasty had in effect transformed the typically continental conception of the Chinese empire into what might be termed a maritime or seagoing conception. Formerly, foreigners voyaging to China had used their own vessels; but, gradually, not a few now began to make use of Chinese ships. Especially during the Sung and Yüan periods, the Arab (*Ta-shih*) merchants preferred to use the Chinese vessels, whose construction and fittings could be considered much better than those of other countries. In their turn the Chinese merchants, under government aegis, began to sail their ships as far as South-East Asia and India, and managed to wrest from their Muslim rivals their monopoly in the carriage of cargoes and passengers.[33]

But China did not limit itself to becoming a mercantile nation; it also became, in the space of a few decades, a maritime nation of the first rank. This Chinese vocation for the sea can be considered more an interlude of a few centuries than a normal development in the history of the Chinese people. Some writers indeed, even in recent times, have insisted that China has never been a maritime power, and that the Chinese people, a people essentially tied to the land, has during the centuries turned its attention more towards the interior of Central Asia than towards the external world, acquiring only a rather limited knowledge of the seas around its coasts.[34]

Certainly, if the term "maritime nation" connotes the possession and use of a naval force able to maintain control and supremacy in the oceans, the China of the period between the Han and T'ang dynasties cannot be regarded as such, notwithstanding its use of naval fleets for coastal warfare and for the invasion of Korea and Indo-China. But its situation changed radically in the late Middle Ages, and in particular in the late Sung and Yüan and early Ming periods.[35]

When the Sung Court was obliged, after its reverse at the hands of the Chin invaders in 1127, to transfer its capital to the coastal city of Hang-chou, which was exposed to attack from the sea, it had to take effective measures against this danger. "The Chinese needed a navy and they succeeded in building a strong and mobile one."[36]

It was thus possible to repel and defeat the dangerous attack of 1161, and later on several occasions to blunt the force of the Mongol offensive. "Built upon the remains of the provincial navy of Northern Sung and favoured by contemporary technological advances in the art of navigation, naval architecture, and the manufacture and use of fire-arms, the Southern Sung navy reached a high degree of efficiency. It won victories when the army suffered setbacks . . . [and it] had the distinction of being the first national navy to be established on a permanent basis and to function as an independent service. In 1130 the Chinese navy already numbered 11 squadrons with 3,000 men. This led to the establishment, two years later, of the Imperial Commissioner's office for the Control and Organization of the Coastal Areas, with its headquarters at Ting-hai, one of the islands of the Chusan group. By 1174 there were 15 squadrons with 21,000 men, and in 1237 the navy could boast a combat force of 20 squadrons with about 52,000 men. The most important naval base was Hsü-pu, on the Yangtse estuary, protecting the flourishing port later to be known as Shanghai. Second in importance was still the base of Ting-hai, set up to defend the capital Hang-chou."[37]

Obviously, such a powerful naval war fleet, with so substantial an organization behind it, was not only a solid bulwark of defence but also conferred an unchallenged prestige on China's constantly growing and wider ranging merchant navy.

III

The Expansion and Deployment of China's Navy

China's peaceful ventures into the exotic world of Africa—a remarkable episode in the history of civilization—were the product of national propensities, of commercial interests, of technical ability and of the nautical knowledge acquired by the Chinese. If even today this nautical knowledge evokes profound admiration, it must have seemed even more prodigious to peoples of long ago, of whatever race or continent.

The big ocean-going junks of the Middle Ages, in their shape, rig and gear, were developed and perfected above all during the two Sung dynasties. One is told of a naval architect who from about AD 600 took in hand the construction of vessels of large tonnage with up to five decks, measuring more than 90 feet from loading deck to keel.

Whereas the seamen of the chronicles and adventure stories of Fa Hsien navigated by the stars, those of the T'ang period also had the advantage of the magnetic compass as a guide; already in the tenth century it had been used in voyages to the southern and western seas. Needham writes: "Although the first clear and datable descriptions of the magnetic compass, with needle, antedate European knowledge of it by one or two centuries . . . it is probable that the Chinese use of the compass-needle is some three or four centuries older."[38]

The rudder at the stern seems to date from the eighth century. Chinese junks generally had sails with two yards, which like modern Western sails allowed them to sail into the wind.[39] It is not known in what period and in what part of the globe this system, of such vital importance for seamen, was first evolved; but it is probable that the Chinese learnt it from ocean peoples, such as the Polynesians, who from time immemorial have used a surprisingly modern rig.[40]

A notable feature of the junks was the scientific cut of the sails: this was convex, as in the modern Bermuda rig; the sail sections were disposed horizontally. The sails themselves were made up of thin strips of bamboo, giving a firmness comparable with modern trends towards stiffer materials.

Marco Polo gives a precise description of the Chinese junks which contains many interesting details. He says, *inter alia*, that they were built of pine; that they had a deck under which were 50 or 60 cabins for the merchants; and that they had a good rudder.[41] They had four masts, with many sails, and some had two auxiliary sails to be hoisted or lowered as required. The hold was divided inside, apart from the cabins, by 13 bulkheads, which had the function of actual watertight compartments which could contain any water that might come into the ship if she ran on to rocks or struck a whale. The larger junks of this kind needed crews of 300 men; others of lesser size required 200 or 150. Marco Polo adds that in earlier times ships were bigger, but storms, rocks and shallow harbours were against them, so that it was decided to build smaller vessels. "The big ships are accompanied by two or three large boats, able to carry about 1,000 sacks of pepper, with crews of 60, 80 or 100 men. They often tow the larger ships, rowing. . . . The big boats in turn have small craft with them."[42] Yule, in *The Book of Marco Polo*, points out that the ships of the China seas in that period were obviously larger than those being used in European waters.[43]

Ibn Battuta visited the Indies in about 1330, or half a century after Marco Polo. He too gives an interesting description of the Chinese ships, of which he met 13 in the port of Calicut. They are, he says, of three types, large, medium and small. The large ones have 12 sails, made of strips of bamboo sewn together to form a sort of material. They need 1,000 men—600 sailors and 400 soldiers—to handle them. They have two stone anchors attached to osier ropes running over a pulley.[44] When there is no wind the crew must take to the oars, and Ibn Battuta speaks of 20 oars, each driven by four men. The big junks are followed by three smaller craft. They are built in the city of Zeitum (presumably the famous port of Zayton or Ch'üan-chou) and also in Syn-Cafan or Canton. Describing the construction of the ships, Ibn Battuta says: "On a ship four decks are built. It [the ship] has cabins, saloons and state rooms for the merchants. The sailors sow pot-herbs and vegetables in wooden buckets. The master of the ship is like a great emir. When he disembarks the archers and the Abyssinians march in front of him with javelins, swords, drums, horns and trumpets."[45]

The Chinese shipyards, as has already been remarked, were from the first centuries AD building ships of three or more masts—such ships as the European maritime powers only contrived in the second half of the fifteenth century for their ocean ventures of discovery and the conquest of new worlds. The Chinese could certainly boast a primacy in the dimensions of their ocean-going junks, as leading modern authorities confirm.

Needham writes that the Chinese vessels were of 700 tons and over, whereas the average for the ships of the Invincible Armada was 528 tons, as against 177 for the vessels of the English fleet.[46] In 1420, under the second Ming Emperor, the building of many-masted ships in China was so widespread as to justify the creation of an appropriate administrative body, known as the *Ta-t'ung-kuan t'i-chü-ssu*, the Ta-t'ung Customs Administration.[47]

However, although quite considerable fleets both in number and size of vessels had been sailing between Canton and the Persian Gulf and Indian and Egyptian ports from remote times, the historians and chroniclers of the first Chinese dynasties have left us very few substantive accounts of naval organization and naval enterprises in their times.[48] As regards the Mediterranean lands and the West in general, towards the end of the thirteenth century and the beginning of the fourteenth the Chinese navy began to become known in Europe through the accounts of Marco Polo. Nor is it to be forgotten that, periods of splendour or decadence apart, there have been from antiquity almost until our own times very few structural changes in Chinese shipbuilding practice (fig. 2).[49]

During the Ming dynasty (1368–1644) a number of Chinese works on naval topics appeared. They included the accounts of the voyages of Cheng Ho, described in a later chapter, and of the naval operations against the Japanese pirates, of which the *Ch'ou-hai t'u-pien* of 1562 may be mentioned.

"The vast size of the Chinese fleet", writes Audemard, "had been proverbial from antiquity down to our own days. To give an idea of the prodigious number of its ships the most ancient chronicles compared them, for numbers, to the leaves of the forest, and for diversity to the manifold plants of China's soil. The poetic image can be rendered more concrete by saying, with many ancient and modern travellers, that there are more ships in China than in all the rest of the world."[50]

Chinese texts relating to Africa, collected and translated into French by Duyvendak and published in 1939, give a clear idea of both the spectacular size and the routes of the fleets of enormous junks which sailed to the remote African shores.[51] Duyvendak's texts are part of a compilation, edited by Youssouf Kamal, printed in the form of a gigantic album whose pages measure 24 inches by nearly 30 inches.

The voyages of these fleets to and from the Muslim lands in the west, like those of the Arabs and Persians themselves to and from the Far East, took a considerable length of time, being determined both by the alternation of the monsoon winds and exigencies of trading. The long months waiting for the homeward monsoon were spent in barter and in acquiring the most desirable of the local products.

The *Ling-wai tai-ta*, written in 1178 by Chou Ch'ü-fei, calculated that a ship that sailed from China in midwinter (eleventh month) would reach Lam-li (Lamri, on the north-western corner of Sumatra) in about 40 days. Here it would trade during the summer; after which, with the monsoon of the following year, it would raise anchor to sail on in 60 days to the land of the Arabs. Thus a whole return voyage would take well over a year. Kuwabara notes that the Arab merchants generally took two years to reach China, trade and return home. "The ships from the southern seas came to China with the south-west wind from the end of the tenth moon to the twelfth moon, so that the half year from May to October was the busiest time at the sea-ports."[52]

The *P'ing-chou k'o-t'an* of Chu Yu states: "All the ocean-going ships set sail in the eleventh or twelfth month, and return with the south wind in the fifth or sixth month."

The problems connected with the long duration of the round voyage of the Chinese fleets have led some scholars, Schwarz for example, to draw some inferences which give rise to interesting but debatable theories. These theories today seem frankly hazardous;[53] but should they be confirmed by new archaeological or ethnological research, or the fortunate discovery of relevant ancient texts, the history of relations between the Far East and Africa might have a new chapter added to it.

Schwarz observes, following the *Book of Marvels of India*, that the Chinese fleet in 945 numbered 1,000 ships under sail. Accepting Ibn Battuta's account, according to which each capital ship was accompanied by three auxiliary craft, the fleet would have consisted of 250 large vessels and 750 smaller, with a total complement of about 250,000 men. It is clear that in the voyages to the western seas and to African shores only a part of the fleet and its complement was engaged. This point Schwarz ignores. But it is easy, from the detailed accounts of the great expeditions of the early Ming period, to establish that the number of ships was not much above 60, nor that of their total complement of men much above 30,000.

Nor is Schwarz much more consistent on the subject of the duration of the voyages. While at the outset he states that the monsoon winds "allowed the junks to come down the coast from October to March, and to return six months later, in both journeys with a wind behind them", he goes on to write that "the voyage took two years, and although there were store ships carrying provisions for the crews of the great junks, there could hardly be enough to last them for the return journey of another two years [sic]."

However, Schwarz maintains that, like the Phoenician sailors who as some claim circumnavigated Africa in the seventh century BC in the reign of the Pharaoh Necho, so too the Chinese stocked up on the African coasts with millet, barley and rice in vast quantities, given the enormous number of mouths to feed.[54]

To continue with Schwarz's hypothesis, in the district of Inyanga near the Rhodesia–Mozambique border, and also on the Usambara plateau south-west of Mombasa, the whole terrain for dozens of square miles is covered with terraced gardens similar to those of China itself. From the plain to the top of the hill the ground is carefully levelled, with strong stone walls following the contours. These walls formerly retained the soil, which centuries of tropical rains have since washed away. "The Chinese, we must suppose, sought out a region free of bush, no matter if it was distant from the coast, for there were porters in plenty to carry the harvest to the ships." Schwarz calculates that the quantity of rice necessary for the round voyage was a good 90,000 tons, with a further 100,000 needed for the six months' stay in Africa and for the rations of the enormous host of labourers. It was to meet these exacting food requirements that the terrace cultivations of Inyanga and Usambara were designed.[55]

Schwarz's entire conception seems to pass from the bounds of reality into the realms of fantasy. It would appear not to have been taken up by Sinologists, nor by other students of African history. Only Fripp, who in 1940 had made some observations on trade between China and Africa in the Middle Ages, returned to the theme again after reading Schwarz's article, and opined that Schwarz's hypothesis could not be accepted. He says it is certainly to be noted that in some areas of eastern Mashonaland African farmers practising terrace cultivation of rice not only grow enough for their own needs but often have rice to offer for sale to Europeans. But Schwarz's theory about Inyanga and Usambara does not seem to be supported by any concrete evidence.[57]

Nor does Schwarz appear to give very convincing answers to the question he asks himself about traces which the Chinese might have left behind them, whether in language, tools, human remains or local traditions that might refer to their passage. Not unjustifiably he considers the Chinese language too difficult for one to expect to find traces of it in these regions. Children born to African women of Chinese fathers would have been born when the Chinese were already homeward bound, after their usual six months' wait for the favourable monsoon, so that they would have had no chance to learn the

2   Chinese junk, early 19th century

赤龍舟圖

3, 4, 5　Various types of ancient Chinese war junks

樓船圖

4

沙船圖

language of their fathers. The explanation is the more conclusive if the Chinese only visited these regions once, instead of maintaining a regular traffic, as Schwarz appears to believe.

As regards the failure to discover Chinese burials in these localities, Schwarz finds this consistent with Chinese customs in all parts of the world, by which any Chinese who died abroad was embalmed and brought home to rest beside his ancestors. "Millions of Chinese", he writes, "must have swarmed over East Africa between 900 and 1200, but they did not leave their dead behind them if they could help it. Some were driven beyond Cape Corrientes and were wrecked, and their descendants live in Africa today, and in West Africa, perhaps, someday, a Chinese grave may be discovered, but on the East Coast never."[58]

As for other remains, such as pottery of various types and periods, specimens found all along the coast are in themselves highly suggestive, Schwarz points out; other finds could be made in the ruins of Inyanga and Usambara if systematic excavation were carried out. As regards oral traditions, Schwarz states that legends are current in Rhodesia about ghosts clad in silk who speak an altogether incomprehensible language.

In short, Schwarz considers that the coast and islands and some interior regions of East Africa were centres of attraction and intense traffic for the Chinese between AD 900 and 1200. Towards 1250, however, they were driven from the Indian Ocean by the Arabs, who from that moment endeavoured to keep every other rival away from Africa's eastern coast. Thus the regular traffic which China had built up ceased, even if individual junks continued to sail to harbours of the Indian Ocean.

In reality, this decline in Chinese-African traffic, attributed by Schwarz to the growing power and enterprise of the Arabs, does not appear to be confirmed by the facts or by the views of competent scholars. The latter, on the contrary, regard the final Sung period, the Yüan period and the early Ming period as constituting three centuries of maritime activity which were to make China a naval power capable of dominating the eastern sea routes as far as Japan and the western as far as the Indian Ocean shores of Africa.[59]

IV

The Earliest Chinese Descriptions of African Countries

The oldest accounts of Western countries to be found in Chinese literature contain no allusions of any kind which can be interpreted as referring to any part of the African continent. No mention of African harbours can be traced to before the beginning of the third century AD; the accounts of them that then reached China have only survived in fairly distorted texts. In particular one may note the reference to the city of Wu-ch'i-san, identifiable as Alexandria in Egypt, contained in the *Wei-lüeh* or *Wei-lio*.

It is in Chinese sources of the T'ang period that one finds the first indisputable accounts of the most remote countries of the West, and hence of Africa.[60] From then on various references by Chinese writers indicate a familiarity with the contacts and commercial exchanges which had been established in the course of centuries between China and the countries of East Africa, known by the name of Tseng-pat or Tseng-po or Ts'ong-pa.

According to Standes, "Chinese authors writing in the 14th century were well acquainted with the export of their country's products [that is, of celadon porcelain] to the coast of Zanzibar, which they called Tsangpat or Tseng-po."[61] Ingrams observes, concerning the description of the country of Ts'ong-pa contained in the *Chu-fan chih* of Chao Ju-kua: "Ts'ong-pa is the Chinese form of Zanzibar. Here the author means not only the island, but the whole of the territory formerly known as Zanguebar" (that is, "land of the blacks").[62]

Towards this part of the world a great fleet sailed every year, first putting in at the harbours of the Persian Gulf and the Arabian peninsula; and when the south-west monsoon started to blow it set sail again for its homeland.

The first Chinese reference to the African continent appears to be that contained in the *Yu-yang tsa-tsu*, written towards the end of the T'ang dynasty by Tuan Chêng-shih, who died in AD 863. It offers us a description of "the country of Bo-ba-li" or "Po-pa-li", identifiable as the region of Berbera and the remaining coastline of the Horn of Africa, with vague allusions to an arid land inhabited by nomad herdsmen (Somali, Galla and perhaps Masai) who were often attacked and raided by the Arabs.[63]

Duyvendak gives the following version of the passage relating to the region of Po-pa-li: "The country of Po-pa-li is in the south-western sea. [The people] do not eat any of the five grains but eat only meat. They often stick a needle into the veins of cattle and draw blood which they drink raw, mixed with milk. They wear no clothes except that they cover [the parts] below their loins with sheepskins. Their women are clean and of proper behaviour. The inhabitants themselves kidnap them, and if they sell them to foreign merchants, they fetch several times their price. The country produces only ivory and ambergris. If Persian merchants wish to go into the country, they collect around them several thousand men and present them with strips of cloth. All, whether old or young, draw blood and swear an oath and then only do they trade their products. From olden times on they were not subject to any foreign country. In fighting they use elephants' tusks and ribs and the horns of wild buffaloes as lances and they wear cuirasses and bows and arrows. They have twenty myriads of foot soldiers. The Arabs make frequent raids upon them."[64]

The antiquity of the *Yu-yang tsa-tsu* is indisputable, even if the text was published much later by Mao Chin (1598–1657) in the *Chin-tai pi-shu*. The most convincing proof of its authenticity is to be found in the *Hsin T'ang-shu* or "New T'ang History", completed by Ou-yang Hsiu in 1060. which recapitulates an extract of the *Yu-yang tsa-tsu* in which the information about Berbera is in part repeated.[65]

But the *Hsin T'ang-shu* also makes brief reference to another African territory not previously mentioned, that of Ma-lin, unmistakably identifiable as Malindi.[66] The passage runs: "South-west from Fu-lin, that is the country of the Roman Orient of which 'Ch'ih-san', Alexandria, is indicated as the western border, after one traverses the desert for two thousand miles is a country called Ma-lin. It is the old P'o-sa. Its people are black and their nature is fierce. The land is pestilentious and has no herbs, no trees, and no cereals. They feed the horses on dried fish; the people eat *hu-mang*; the hu-mang is the Persian date. They are not ashamed of debauching the wives of their fathers or chiefs, they are [in this respect] the worst of the barbarians. They call this: to seek out the proper master and subject In the seventh moon they rest completely [i.e. Ramadan]. They [then] do not send out nor receive [any merchandise] in trade and they sit drinking all night long."

Somewhat fuller, containing interesting additional details, is the description of Bo-ba-li given in the *Chu-fan-chih* or "Description of

Barbarian Peoples" compiled in 1226, on the basis of earlier sources, by Chao Ju-kua, already mentioned above, who (according to Hirth and Rockhill) was a descendant of the Emperor Tai-tsung and Inspector of Foreign Trade (*Shih-po-ssu*) at Chüan-chou in Fukien.[67] This post provided him with opportunities for collecting a great deal of information at first hand from traders and from foreigners.

The Chu-fan-chih, in its two parts, is a real inventory—strangely arranged as it may be—of foreign countries, and of foreign products; from the East Indies archipelago, the Malay peninsula, India and the Arab lands to the peoples of the eastern coast of Africa and of the Mediterranean.

Among the lands subject to the country of the Ta-shih or Arabs (Part I, 22) are named and described the countries of Ts'eng-pa, or Zanzibar (Part I, 24) and of Pi-p'a-lo. or the coast of Berbera (Part I, 25). There is then a description of the country of Chung-li, or the Somali coast (Part I, 27), while under "Countries situated in the sea" is mentioned the country of Kan-mei (which might be the Comoro islands). Also described are the K'un-lun-ts'eng-ch'i islands, or Pemba and Madagascar (Part I, 38, 2) and Wu-ssu-li or Misr, Egypt (Part I, 36) with the city of O-ken-t'o or Alexandria (Part I, 37) and the country of Mo-ch'ieh-lao or Maghrib al-'aqsa (Part I, 38, 8). Of Pi-no-yeh, corresponding to Libya, only the name is given.[68]

In the description of Wu-ssu-li or Misr (Egypt) the narrative dwells on the figure of the king, on the administrative division of the country, on its natural resources, on the foods eaten by its inhabitants, and on its fauna. It also speaks of a strange being who rises every two or three years from the waters of a river, and to whom the people address themselves to know if the coming year will be one of prosperity or misfortune; the answer, in either sense, being conveyed by the river deity laughing or grunting as the case might be.[69] The description of O-kent'o or Alexandria speaks of a great tower, which perhaps is the Pharos or lighthouse built by Alexander of Macedon.[70]

From the chronicle's account of the country of Ts'eng-pa or Zanzibar one learns that, going westwards across the country. one comes to a great mountain, perhaps identifiable as Kilimanjaro, whose existence the subjects of the Zinj sultan, Sulayman Hasan, must have discovered in the second half of the twelfth century.[71]

Chao Ju-kua tells us: "The Ts'ong-pa country is on an island of the sea south of Hu-ch'a-la. To the west it reaches to a great mountain. The inhabitants are of Ta'shi stock and follow the Ta'shi religion. They wrap themselves in blue foreign cotton stuffs, and wear red leather shoes. Their daily food consists of meal, baked cakes and mutton. There are many villages, and a succession of wooded hills and terraced rocks. The climate is warm, and there is no cold season. The products of the country consist of elephants' tusks, native gold, ambergris and yellow sandalwood. Every year Hu-ch'a-la and the Ta'shi localities along the sea coast send ships to this country, with white cotton cloths, porcelain, copper and red cotton to trade." Ingrams adds by way of explanation: "Tsang-pa is the Chinese form of Zanzibar. Here the author means not only the island, but the whole of the territory formerly known as Zanguebar. Hu-ch'a-la is Gujerat and the Ta'shi are Arabs. The great mountain is probably Kilimanjaro."[72]

Probsthain's *Catalogue of Chinese Art* reproduces, among the paintings of scenes taken from the "Strange and Curious Lands", a picture attributed to Li Lung-mien, the most celebrated painter of the Sung dynasty, which represents the country of K'un lun. In the chapter referring to the writings of the Arab geographers, Kambalu (of which K'un lun is the Chinese form) is identified with Mkumbuu on the island of Pemba,[73] so that Li Ling-mien's picture would convey the idea which the Chinese had of Pemba in the eleventh century (Li Lung-mien lived from 1049 until perhaps 1104).

Chao Ju-kua, in the section "Countries situated in the sea" in the Chu-fan-chih, gives the following description of K'un-lun-ts'eng-ch'i: "This country is in the south-west. It is adjacent to a large island (probably Madagascar). There are usually three great p'öng birds which so mask the sun in their flight that the shade on the sundial is shifted. If the great p'öng bird finds a wild camel it swallows it, and if one should chance to find a p'öng's feather he can make a water butt of it, after cutting off the hollow quill. The products of the country are big elephants' tusks and rhinoceros horns. In the west there is an island in the sea on which there are many savages, with bodies as black as lacquer and with frizzled hair. They are enticed by [offers of] food, then caught and carried off for slaves to the Ta'shi countries where they fetch a high price. They are used as gate-keepers."[74]

Coupland observes: "There is no evidence that the Arab slave-traders found large markets for their wares farther east than India; but a number of Africans were probably shipped to China. In 976 a great sensation was produced at the court of the Tang emperor by the arrival of an Arab envoy with a 'negro slave' in his suite; and after that date Chinese books repeatedly refer to 'negro slaves' and, as has already been noticed, to the Arab Slave Trade which produced them. But it seems probable that China absorbed only a small fraction of the vast host of slaves which Asia, century after century, was steadily filching away from Africa."[75]

Duyvendak furnishes further information on this point, from the evidence of Chinese texts. Quoting Chou Ch'ü-fei for the statement that "thousands of them are sold as foreign slaves", he affirms his certainty that some of these slaves reached China. They were known by various names, some indicating their place of origin: thus there was the *K'un-lun-nu*, "slave from K'un-lun", the *Seng-chih-nu*, "slave from Seng-chih", etc. The slaves also had various epithets attached to them, being known as *kuei-nu*, "devil slaves"; *yeh-jen*, "wild men"; *hei-hsiao-ssu*, "black servants"; *fan-hsiao-ssu*, "barbarian servants"; and *fan-nu*, "barbarian slaves". Duyvendak also states that the last consort of the Emperor Chien-wen of the Chin dynasty was nick-named K'un-lun by the courtiers because she was tall and of a dark colour.[76]

The *P'ing-chou k'o-t'an* of Chu Yu (see reference 17) states: "In Kuang-chou most of the wealthy people keep devil-slaves. They are very strong and can lift [weights of] several hundred catties. Their language and tastes are unintelligible. Their nature is simple and they do not run away. They are also called 'wild men'. Their colour is black as ink, their lips are red and their teeth white, their hair is curly and yellow. There are males and females. . . . They live in the mountains (or islands) beyond the seas. They eat raw things. If, in captivity, they are fed on cooked food, after several days they get diarrhoea . . . and sometimes fall ill and die; if they do not die one can keep them, and after having been kept a long time they begin to understand people's language, although they themselves cannot speak it."

Chao Ju-kua also relates that for a boy three taels of gold were paid, or the equivalent in scented wood, and that the slaves were also used on ships to repair leaks underwater.[77] "There is a strange pathos in the thought of these melancholy, silent, black slaves, who were supposed to have no longing for their home, in medieval China, used as doorkeepers."[78]

Late Chinese chroniclers and historians were certainly not averse to reproducing in whole or in part more ancient chronicles or texts. While the *Hsin T'ang-shu* reproduced a condensation of the *Yu-yang tsa-tsu*, one can find in the *Chu-fan-chih* much material taken from the *Ling-wai tai-ta* written about half a century earlier by Chou Ch'ü-fei. Of great interest are the accounts given in this work of the country of Pi-p'a-lo (Berbera); they give us the first descriptions of African animals such as the ostrich, the zebra and above all the giraffe, objects of such delight for the Chinese Imperial Court:

"The country of Pi-pa-lo has four chou [departmental cities] and for the rest [the people] are all settled in villages which each try to gain the supremacy over the others by violence. They serve Heaven and do not serve the Buddha (presumably meaning that they are

Mohammedans). The country produces many camels and sheep (*mien-yang*) and they have camels' meat and milk as well as baked cakes as their regular food. The country produces dragons' saliva (ambergris), big elephants' tusks, and big rhinoceros horns. Some elephants' tusks weigh more than 100 catty and some rhinoceros horns more than 10 catty. There is also much putchuk (*mu-hsiang*), liquid storax gum, myrrh and tortoise-shell which is extremely thick, and which [people from] other countries all come to buy. 'Among the products there is further the so-called camel-crane (i.e. the ostrich, called by the Persians *ushtumurgh* and by the Arabs *tayr al-jamal*, both meaning "camel bird"), whose body to the crown is six or seven feet high. It has wings and can fly, but not to any height' (passage quoted from the *Ling-wai-tai-ta*). Among quadrupeds there is the so-called *tsu-la* (giraffe), striped like a camel and in size like an ox. It is yellow in colour. Its front legs are five feet high and its hind legs are only three feet. Its head is high up and is turned upwards. Its skin is an inch thick. There is also a mule with red, black and white stripes wound as girdles around the body. Both [these kinds] are animals of the mountain wilds. They are occasional variations of the camel. The inhabitants are fond of hunting and from time to time they catch them with poisoned arrows."[79]

Of another region, near Pi-pa-lo, Chou Ch'ü-fei has left us a detailed and lively description, of which Duyvendak gives the following vivid rendering: "The inhabitants of Chung-li go bare-headed and barefoot. They wrap a cloth around themselves but they do not wear jackets. Only ministers and the King's courtiers wear jackets and turbans on their heads as a mark of distinction. The king's residence is masoned out of large bricks and slabs of stone; the people's houses are made of palm leaves and are covered with thatch. Their daily fare consists of baked flour-cakes, sheep's and camel's milk. Cattle, sheep, and camels are plentiful, and their 'big food' (that is food eaten on special occasions) is only this. The country produces frankincense. Many people are [addicted to] magical tricks; they can change their bodies into the shapes of birds and beasts or aquatic animals, and they frighten or bewilder the ignorant people. If in their commercial dealings with a foreign ship there may occasionally be a quarrel, they (the sorcerers) pronounce a ban over it so that the ship can neither move backward nor forward, and not until (the participants in the quarrel) have been wise enough to settle the dispute is it released. [The government of] the country has strictly forbidden this.

"Every year countless numbers of birds of passage alight outside the suburbs. As soon as the sun rises they disappear without a trace. The inhabitants catch them with nets and eat them; their taste is delicious. They appear only towards the end of spring, and when summer comes they disappear until the following year, when they appear again.

"When one of the inhabitants dies, and when, the body having been placed in the coffin, they are about to bury him, the kinsmen from far and near come to condole. All of them swinging swords go in and ask the chief mourner the cause of the death. 'If he was killed by the hand of man' (they say) 'we shall kill the murderer in revenge with this sword.' If the chief mourner replies that [the deceased] was not killed by anybody, but that it was a natural result of Heaven's decree, then they throw down their swords and burst into violent wailing.

"Every year regularly big, dead fish are driven on the neighbouring coast; they are more than 200 feet in length and 20 feet high in diameter. The inhabitants do not eat their flesh, but they cut away their brains and marrow as well as their eyes to make oil, as much as more than 300 teng (Skr. tola, a weight equal to 4 mashas). They mix this oil with lime to caulk their boats or use it for lamps. The poor people use the ribs of these fish to make rafters for their huts, and the back-bones for door-leaves, and they cut off the vertebrae to fashion them into mortars.

"The country has mountains which are contiguous with Pi-pa-lo (Berbera). In circumference it is about 4,000 li;[80] for the most part it is not populated. The mountains produce dragon's blood and aloes, and the waters [of the sea] produce tortoise-shell and ambergris. It is not known where the ambergris comes from; suddenly it appears in lumps, sometimes 3–5, sometimes 10 catties in weight, driven on the shore by the wind. The natives vie with one another in dividing it. Sometimes a ship at sea runs across it and picks it up."[81]

Hirth and Rockhill would see in this country northern Somalia or the island of Socotra, to the east of Cape Guardafui, while Duyvendak rules the latter out since the text refers explicitly to mountains on the borders of the region of Pi-pa-lo. What must surely be intended is the territory stretching from Berbera to the mountainous ridges of Migiurtinia. As for the stories of wizards and the references to catching whales and the use of parts of them to repair boats or to build the frames of huts, these are tales which are found in Arab writers like Al-Idrisi, and in Marco Polo.

To sum up, one can deduce that between the tenth and fourteenth centuries the knowledge of Chinese geographers and chroniclers was not limited only to these northern regions of the Horn of Africa, but extended also to the south of Cape Guardafui and Ras Hafun, where "the land of the Berbera", i.e. the Somalis, ended and the land of Azania or the Zinj began.[82] In any case, this name must

6   Painting of the giraffe sent to the Chinese court from Bengal. The painting
     was discovered by Professor Duyvendak in New York (see reference 99)

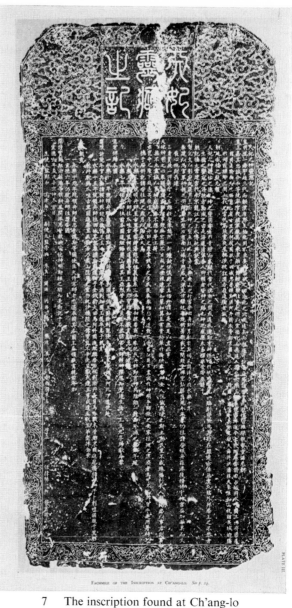

FACSIMILE OF THE INSCRIPTION AT CH'ANG-LO. *See p. 24.*

7   The inscription found at Ch'ang-lo

already have been known in China in the ninth century because of the Arab and Persian merchants getting the Bantu slaves there that have already been referred to.

Moreover, there can be no doubt that the Chinese navigators contrived to trace the routes of their voyages on maps which at the outset were pretty imperfect, but which gradually became more exact with new knowledge and fresh observations. In other words, they continued to compare and correct their maps, on which were marked courses plotted by the compass and by the stars, showing the configuration of the coasts and the islands, and also any special features of the waters traversed.[83] One had therefore real nautical charts which identified the various points of the coast important for navigators. So far as concerns Africa, as Duyvendak says, "they carry us all the way to the African coast". One finds rather surprisingly, however, the account given by Fuchs, in his observations on Chu Ssu-pen's Mongol Atlas of China, of a map of c. 1300 in which Africa's triangular outline is already delineated.[84]

V

China's Westward Ventures in the Early Ming Period

The resistance of the Southern Sung dynasty to the pressure of the Mongol invaders ended in final collapse when the Mongols, having caused the death at sea of the last imperial prince Ti-ping, stormed across the Great Wall in 1280 and installed the first foreign dynasty (1280–1367). However, this long interlude in Chinese history by no means had the effect of drying up the lively traffic between East and West which famous travellers like Marco Polo and Ibn Battuta, or ardent preachers like Giovanni da Montecorvino and Odorico, were to represent so vividly in their chronicles, offering us the picture of a fabulous world, open to foreigners in all its aspects.[85]

The Mongol invaders, in fact, were soon fired by the Sung example to make the navy an instrument of expansion and conquest. Within the space of a few decades these warriors, used only to travelling on horseback and having no nautical knowledge or experience, had become able to contest the seas not only with China but with all the other countries of the Asiatic Far East. Partly by their own ship-building efforts, and partly through their captures of enemy vessels, the Mongols succeeded in assembling a fair number of warships; and once they had overcome the Sung resistance, having destroyed the enemy's remaining fleet at the battle of Yai-shan in 1279, they embarked on a gigantic naval construction programme[86] which engaged the most distant shipyards of the vast Mongol empire.

Then, in the middle of the fourteenth century, the bonze Chu Yüan-chang launched a resolute struggle for the liberation of his country from the Mongol Yüan dynasty. It was crowned with complete success. Changing his monk's habit for a soldier's cloak, this man of humble origin succeeded in driving the enemy from the country and founding the Ming dynasty, of which he was the first emperor, giving the years of his reign the name of *hung-wu*.[87]

The collapse of the vast empire created by the Mongols naturally faced the Chinese liberators with exacting problems of reorganization in many fields, including that of foreign trade; there had been a temporary stoppage in the influx of the exotic products which China was now accustomed to getting.

The importance of trade with the outside world was regarded differently by the responsible Chinese quarters according to whether it was looked at from the practical or the ethical point of view. From the practical standpoint, as Duyvendak points out, foreign trade meant prosperity for an infinite number of people who derived profit from it. The import dues went to swell the funds of the public treasury, and although, as we have seen, the export of coin was considered definitely harmful, the advantages of this commerce, especially for the southern provinces, was substantial. From the ethical and ideological standpoint, on the other hand, this kind of traffic had never been admitted; in Confucian doctrine trade was regarded as something mean and almost sordid, which the Emperor as such should never have had anything to do with. For this reason, relations with overseas foreign countries were always presented in the form of payment of tribute and thereby of homage done by remote barbarian countries to the Son of Heaven, in acknowledgment of his omnipotence. After this, as a mark of benevolence, these foreigners were graciously permitted to conduct their trade with China.[88]

This procedure had been followed by the previous dynasties also; they had sent embassies to the southern and western seas seeking to persuade distant nations to bring their humble tribute, with which they would augment the prestige of the Chinese Emperors and improve their own. Indeed, the more foreign envoys could take part in the solemn Court audiences on the occasion of the New Year the more lustre was added to the glory of the Son of Heaven.

"These mixed motives: the real need of overseas products felt particularly at Court, and the desire to increase his own prestige and re-establish the overseas renown of the Chinese Empire, must have prompted the third Emperor of the Ming dynasty to undertake a series of missions overseas. In the official Annals still another motive is adduced, namely, a political one. The Yung-lo Emperor, son of the founder, only gained the throne by deposing his young nephew, to whom the throne had been bequeathed. The nephew disappeared: it was rumoured that he had fled overseas, and therefore a fleet was sent out to try and bring him back from the countries of the barbarians, where he was supposed to be hiding. The excuse is transparent; for such a purpose it would not have been necessary to undertake expeditions on such a scale as sailed, not merely once, but at least seven times, not counting minor ones. Some of them comprised no less than sixty-two vessels carrying 37,000 soldiers; more than thirty countries in the Indian Archipelago and the Indian Ocean were visited, and besides ports in the Persian Gulf, places like Aden and Mecca were visited and the Chinese ships sailed all the way to Africa."[89]

Needham's observations on the subject were not very dissimilar from Duyvendak's. Speaking of Cheng Ho's voyage he says: "The reasons for these expeditions are not known; they may have been intended to counterbalance the foreign trade which had now dried up over the land routes, or to increase the grandeur of the imperial court, or even, as the official Annals said, to seek out the emperor's predecessor and nephew (who, in fact, had disappeared underground as a Buddhist monk and was found many years later in a succeeding reign)."[90]

The same arguments are put by Cordier: "With the object of enhancing China's prestige in foreign lands, and also no doubt in order to look for traces of the preceding Emperor, Chien-wen Ti, who had mysteriously disappeared, Yung-lo, after sending other expeditions to Java, Sumatra and Bengal in the first year of his reign, dispatched the eunuch Cheng Ho, a distinguished soldier known under the name of San-pao t'ai-chien,[91] to the countries of the Western Ocean. He took 62 ships, mostly vessels of big tonnage, with 37,000 soldiers and gifts of gold and silk."[92]

The versions of Duyvendak, Needham and Cordier also accord with the account given in the *Li-tai t'ung-chien chi-lan* (Essentia Historiae), compiled and published by Lu Hsi-hsiung, who died in 1767. This gives the following summary of Cheng Ho's ventures in the western seas: "In the third year of the reign of Yung-lo (1405) the eunuch Cheng Ho, commonly known as 'The Eunuch of the Three Jewels', a native of the province of Yunnan, was sent on a mission to the Western Ocean. The Emperor, suspecting that the last Emperor of the Yüan dynasty might have fled beyond the seas, charged Cheng Ho, Wang Ching-hung and others with following his traces. Taking with them a large quantity of gold and other treasures, and with a force of more than 37,000 soldiers under their command, they built great ships, 62 in number, and set sail from Liu-chia Chiang[93] in the prefecture of Suchow, from where they sailed by Kukien to Chan-Ch'êng, and from there [undertook] voyages across the Western seas. Here they made known the decrees of the Son of Heaven and spread in foreign lands the knowledge of his majesty and benevolence. They bestowed gifts on kings and governors, and all who offered opposition they compelled by force to submit. Every country [thus] became obedient to the imperial orders, and when Cheng Ho returned home he brought with him envoys to offer tribute. The Emperor was extremely pleased, and not long after ordered Cheng Ho to go again beyond the seas to spread bounty among the various states. In this way the number of those presenting themselves before the throne became ever greater. Cheng Ho was entrusted with not less than seven missions, and three times he took foreign rulers captive. His successes were such as had never been equalled by any other eunuch before him since the remotest times. At the same time various peoples, attracted by the profits in Chinese commodities, extended their intercourse for the purpose of trade, and there was continued movement to and fro. Thus it happened that in those days 'The Eunuch of the Three Jewels Going Down to the West' became a proverbial expression. . . ."

According to a passage in the biography of Cheng Ho, the decision of the Emperor Yung-lo was motivated on the one hand by the desire to recover the traces of his predecessor Chien-wen Ti whom he considered to have "disappeared beyond the seas", and on the other by the desire to "achieve military successes in foreign countries and show that China was rich and powerful".[94]

As regards the Emperor Yung-lo's decision that these expeditions should also visit the African coasts, some consider that it was inspired by an earlier initiative of the Sultan of Malindi[95] who in 1415 sent an embassy to the Chinese Emperor with various gifts, among them a magnificent specimen of a giraffe.

In the division and classification of Birds and Reptiles in the *T'u-shu chi-ch'eng* (chapter 56, section on "ch'i-lin", pp. 27b–31b) one reads: "In the autumn of the 12th year of Yung-lo the country of Bengal came to Court and presented a *ch'i-lin*. In the autumn of the same year the country of Melinda (Malindi) came again to present a *ch'i-lin*."[96]

Duyvendak points out that Bengal is not a country whose natural fauna includes giraffe, so that it must have come from elsewhere. He thinks that the solution to the enigma is to be found in the fact that the African country of Malindi, with which China had previously had no relations, was suddenly found appearing at Court bringing a giraffe in homage. "I believe that what happened is this: we know that in Bengal there just was a new king, Saifu'd-Din, who on ascending the throne, naturally received presents from various Mohammedan, including African, countries. Among these presents must have been giraffes, one of which passed on to the Chinese Emperor, and the Chinese must have met the Ambassadors from Melinda and given them a hint that such an animal would be a very welcome gift at court. The result was that the following year Melinda came to present a giraffe."

When the giraffe arrived the Emperor "went out to the Feng-t'ien gate to receive the animal in great state, together with a 'celestial horse' (zebra) and a 'celestial stag' (oryx?), and all the officials prostrated themselves and offered congratulations". But "these ambassadors had to be conducted home, and thus we see that on the fifth voyage (1417–19) for the first time the itinerary is extended all the way to Melinda. It was the giraffe, therefore, that caused the Chinese to sail to Africa."[97]

This conclusion, plausible and suggestive as it may be, is not shared by scholars like Jung-pang Lo, who finds it far-fetched. Jung-pang Lo observes: "One conventional explanation has been that the expeditions were the work of palace attendants designed to bring back rare and precious objects to please the Emperor's fancy and, as such, they were opposed by the scholar-officials. Duyvendak went so far as to suggest that it was to obtain giraffes that the Chinese established contact with East Africa."[98]

In evidence of the effect produced at Court by the apparition of this singular animal, one may recall a congratulatory composition on the occasion of the arrival of the Bengal giraffe, which figures in the *Shu-yü chou-tzu-lu* (chapter 9, pp. 6a and 17a). The author relates that "in the ninth month, in autumn, of the year chia-wu of Yung-lo (1414) a barbarian country of the south-west called Bengal presented a ch'i-lin as tribute. In the following year, yi-wei, in the autumn, in the ninth month, a country called Melinda presented a *ch'i-lin* as tribute. In the same year, in autumn, the country called Aden presented a *ch'i-lin* as tribute." The author describes the "gentle animal, with its strange shape and marvellous structure", its graceful walk and the musical accents of its voice.[99] The apparition of such a creature could be considered as a manifestation from Heaven, and the Emperor received it in the Hall of Receptions. "Thus it happened", Duyvendak remarks, "that the giraffe from the African wilderness, as it strode into the Emperor's Court, became the emblem of Perfect Virtue, Perfect Government, and Perfect Harmony in the Empire and in the Universe."[100]

Inspired by the Chinese writer's eulogy and Duyvendak's remarks on the subject, Italiaander observes: "This giraffe seems to have represented the most sensational salutation from the Africa of that time to contemporary Asia. It was not only presented to the Emperor on a dragon throne and with sumptuous ceremonial, but received almost divine honours. Professor Duyvendak takes the view that this giraffe evoked an atmosphere of myth around it, like the mythical unicorn. Poets celebrated it, artists painted it, and philosophers introduced this miraculous animal into their learned discourses; the giraffe became the symbol of perfect virtue, perfect government and the perfect harmony of the universe. But this giraffe, coming from eastern Africa, brought harm also. It disturbed people's minds, and the Chinese seemed no longer satisfied with what they had at home; perhaps they conceived the desire to know the country from which so many envoys came, the mysterious country in eastern Africa where similar marvellous animals lived."[101]

A long time before these embassies came to the Court with their giraffes from Bengal and from the much more remote countries of Africa, there was a similar initiative which is mentioned in the Annals of the Sung dynasty of 1083. These refer to the visit paid to the Imperial Palace by a foreign envoy, the last letters of whose name can be identified with the word *Zanj*. According to these Annals, the ambassador came from a country so distant that the Emperor, moved by the courage of such an enterprise, added two thousand ounces of silver to the gifts he had already offered.[102]

According to a theory held by Duyvendak (which does not conflict with the two inscriptions of Cheng Ho discovered and published between 1935 and 1937) the clever eunuch, wanting to gratify the Emperor's *amour propre* and ambition by presenting to him the homage of ambassadors from afar, invited traders or notables from the African coasts who were present in the port of Hormuz at the entrance to the Persian Gulf to embark on his ships with an attractive selection of their most typical or most valuable goods and with some animals little known or at any rate rare in China, like the giraffe.

"I rather think", writes Duyvendak, "that the first 'representatives' of these distant places who came to Court sometimes were not real 'ambassadors' at all, but merchants who, with the knowledge and connivance of Cheng Ho and his associates, presented themselves as envoys. It was in Cheng Ho's interest to be able to produce as many foreign ambassadors as possible to the greater flattery of the Emperor and also to extend his trade-relations. For the native merchants the latter consideration must have been decisive. . . . Naturally they must have been offered passage on Chinese ships. . . . The inevitable delay for the various embassies in collecting their 'rare birds and strange animals' and other tribute-articles and getting ready to start, would explain why they did not arrive until late in 1416." Thus "conducting the first merchant(?)-ambassadors home" furnished the opportunity for the fifth voyage which carried Cheng-Ho's fleet to Africa.[103]

If one accepts these interpretations of Duyvendak and other Western scholars, China's direct contacts with Africa originated from quite chance motivations. The more recent arguments of Chinese scholars, however, are very different; for them the phenomenon of China's maritime expansion between the twelfth and the first part of the fifteenth century is not an extravagant episode in the history of its people but a real period of naval supremacy of the Chinese empire in the commercial field as well as the military.

"The creation of the Southern Sung navy", Jung-pang Lo writes, "is said to have stemmed from seaborne commerce, both legitimate and illicit, the overseas campaigns of the Yüan period from the ambition of Qubilai Qan, and the naval expeditions of early Ming from the efforts of Cheng Ho or a group of court attendants to please the emperor by bringing back rare objects from abroad. In the opinion of this writer, the causes were more profound and funda-mental and included economic and social forces, the will of the people and the character of the governments, knowledge of nautical techniques and a naval tradition.[104]

"As the Yüan inherited the Sung navy so the Ming inherited the Yüan navy. Thus the spirit and tradition of the Sung navy were carried on by the two succeeding dynasties. From a defensive arm the navy developed into an instrument of aggression and political domin-ation, and from the East China Sea the naval power of the Chinese advanced to the South China Sea and into the Indian Ocean."[105]

Elsewhere Jung-pang Lo observes: "During the first quarter of the fifth century when China attained short-lived prominence as a major sea power in the Orient it was the culmination of three centuries of maritime activities. The advance out to the sea began in the Southern Sung period when Chinese fleets gained control over the East China Sea, grew in the Yüan period when China achieved ascendancy over the South China Sea, and climaxed in the early Ming period when Chinese warships entered and cruised about the Indian Ocean in demonstration of China's military might, giving China, for a brief span, hegemony over a vast arc of land that extended from Japan to the east coast of Africa. This spectacular expansion was the result of the opportune conjuncture of a number of circumstances, the momentum of the shift of economic and population centres to the south-eastern coastal provinces, the intellectual and cultural flowering which stimulated the spirit of adventure and enterprise; the widening of geographical knowledge and the remarkable development in the techniques of ship-building and the art of navigation; the interest of the state in economic ventures coupled with the growth of money economy and the rise of an influential merchant group which furthered seaborne commerce; and, finally, the almost incessant wars which spurred the invention and manufacture of arms for fighting on land and on water. These conditions, which favoured the movement out to sea and the building of naval forces during the Sung and Yüan periods, persisted in the first decades of the Ming period."[106]

The first Ming Emperor, Hung-wu, was profoundly conscious of the importance of naval power, and Yung-lo, having inherited a strong navy from his father, further reinforced it and used it as an instrument of his policy of overseas expansion. Served by energetic and capable officials, these two monarchs built an efficient navy of 3,500 ships for operating in China's coastal waters. Of these, 2,700—half of them warships and half reconnaissance craft—belonged to the guard stations, 400 were fleet warships based at Hsin-chiang-k'ou near Nanking, and 400 were armed transports of the grain conveyance fleet.[107]

But the pride of the Ming navy was a fleet of over 250 "jewel ships" (pao-ch'uan), each able to carry 500 men; the average burden of such vessels, and thus Cheng Ho's fleet, was reckoned to be about 2,000 *liao*, or 500 tons.[108]

If, as some have sought to argue, China did not actually reach the point of using foreign commerce as an instrument to extract riches from other countries, it undoubtedly used it as an instrument to enrich itself. This concept was asserted and put into practice first by the Sung Emperors Hung-wu and Yung-lo, who even in official declarations encouraged foreign countries to enter into commercial relations with China.[109]

It is a fact that the bulk of the imports which flowed in as tribute or as merchandise in the wake of the imperial envoys were products which China needed, and not simply luxury goods; they were "horses, copper ores, sulphur, timber, hides, drugs, and spices, not to mention gold, silver and rice. In return for the official tribute, the Ming court gave gifts that had greater prestige than intrinsic value, such as suits of clothing, umbrellas and coverlets, embroideries and utensils, calendars and books. Even the 'gold seals' of office were actually silver washed in gold. . . . The advantages of the trade were, thus, chiefly on the side of the Ming court."[110] All the other objects of a frivolous character were secondary in importance.

It is also noteworthy that at this period the bulk of payments or subventions or largesse in cash were effected in paper money,[111] which set a premium on cash and ensured China a favourable balance of trade. This was of course a reflection of its military power and political prestige, and of the soundness of the monetary system during the early Ming period. In view of the lucrative nature of this foreign trade one can understand why the state, to preserve its monopoly and to prevent competition, imposed embargoes on emigration and private trade. "The heyday of the Arab and Persian merchants had passed, the Portuguese had not yet arrived, and thus, for a century, the Chinese controlled all the commerce in the waters of the East."[112]

There have been and still are many conflicting views about the role of the eunuchs in these important initiatives.

In the past, overseas expeditions to foreign countries had been entrusted to various eunuchs. The voyages they directed in the reign of the Emperor Wu in the first century BC (see pages 4 and 5) are a clear demonstration of the continuity of Chinese institutions, a continuity which means that a given historical fact of a thousand years earlier or a thousand years later can be presented and interpreted in its proper terms.

Just as had happened with the eunuchs of fifteen centuries earlier, so Cheng Ho and his companions were put in command of a whole series of expeditions which had the precise aim, *inter alia*, of replenishing the Court's supply of luxury goods and precious commodities. This also explains (despite the contrary opinion of scholars such as Jung-pang Lo) the title of *San-pao t'ai-chien*, "Eunuch of the Three Jewels", given to Cheng Ho, and the name of *pao-ch'uan*, "jewel ships", assigned to the vessels of the fleet which were entrusted to his command. "If I may say so," remarks Duyvendak, "he went a-shopping for the ladies of the Imperial harem."[113]

Certainly, among all the eunuchs to whom from remote times distant missions had been entrusted, the name of Cheng Ho, for the grandiose scale and importance of his exploits, was destined to pass into history as by far the best known, despite the later hostility to him of official circles at Court, which in keeping with the new anti-expansionist trends tried to wipe out every remembrance of the Grand Eunuch.[114]

Pending new researches which may throw light on the influence exercised at Court by this class of Imperial servants, brief mention may be made of views currently held by scholars on this matter. Duyvendak, speaking in general, affirms that during the Ming dynasty there was strong rivalry between the higher imperial bureaucracy and the eunuchs, who "were privately employed by the Emperor in various important functions. This was very galling to the official classes who, anyway, as good Confucianists, despised trade and luxury and looked down upon foreign barbarians."[115] Thus the whole complex of business dealings with foreign countries was regarded by the higher bureaucracy, from the ethical and political standpoint, as closely connected with the intolerable extravagance and thrustfulness of the hated eunuchs.

However, this account of the matter can hardly be accepted as valid for all periods without reservations. Such reservations must be made particularly for the early Ming period and, more precisely, the reigns of the first two Emperors Hung-wu and Yung-lo. One need only recall that the founder of the Ming dynasty held strictly to the policy of keeping down the number of eunuchs at Court, threatening them with execution whenever they interfered in the affairs of government. However, they grew rapidly in numbers and influence under the second Emperor Yung-lo, who began to use them fairly generally for special commissions outside the Imperial Palace. The voyages of Cheng Ho are themselves a result of this trend, which made the eunuchs a dominant factor in Ming political history.[116]

As Jung-pang convincingly argues, it cannot be supposed that the great expeditions carried out under the Emperor Yung-lo could have been the product of the eunuchs' own spirit of enterprise and intrusiveness and could have been put into effect without or against the counsel of official Court circles. "Actually, despite everything that has been written about the baleful influence of the eunuchs, it is doubtful if these palace attendants could, by themselves, have launched the expeditions. Ship-building, navigation, commercial practices and knowledge of foreign lands were the legacies of past centuries and the far-ranging voyages were the expression of a popular urge to expand carried forward by the impetus of a seaward thrust that began in the Sung period or even earlier. Expeditions of the magnitude of those which sailed forth during the Yung-lo period could not have been launched without a measure of support of the officials nor in the face of determined opposition from them. After all, the dispatch of diplomatic and commercial missions abroad was an established practice and, although they were on much grander scale, the Cheng Ho expeditions were official missions no less and they did redound in glory for China.

"Nor," Jung-pang Lo continues, "were only eunuchs sent; many of the envoys were officials.[117] Cheng Ho, though a eunuch, was chosen for his proven ability, and since he and his associates were seldom in the capital there was little occasion for feuds to arise between them and the officials. On the contrary, he was friendly with many of the high officials, respected by them, and contemporary accounts generally depicted him and his overseas activities in a favourable light."[118]

If there was lack of sympathy and open hostility towards the eunuchs, it was not the pattern during the first decades of the Ming dynasty, but only when, later, the eunuchs really began to abuse their functions and commit every sort of peculation and malpractice. This can be said to have begun during the minority of the Emperor Cheng-t'ung (1436–49) when the eunuch Weng Cheng "came to be the evil genius at court and the first of a succession of powerful eunuchs who dominated the political scene. They terrorized, persecuted, arrested, humiliated, tortured, executed and banished officials who criticized or opposed them. . . ."[119]

In this period the eunuchs secured the control of the secret police, the army and the treasury, using them to entrench themselves in power and to accumulate considerable private fortunes by extortion and every other means.

By then, however, the period of great expansion and spectacular overseas ventures was ended, and China's great navy was entering on a rapid and dismal decline.

VI

Chinese Accounts of Brava,
Giumbo and Mogadishu

Rockhill and Hirth[120] list the following as the works which, known to Chinese during the late Yüan dynasty and the early Ming, between the mid-fourteenth and mid-fifteenth centuries, give the basic accounts of voyages to lands in or near the south-east Asian archipelago, in southern Asia and in eastern Africa (Rockhill and Hirth's study was, of course, prior to the researches of Pelliot and Duyvendak and the discovery of the two interesting inscriptions placed by Cheng Ho, the first on 14th March 1431 in the temple of T'ien-fei, the Celestial Spouse, at Liu-chia-chang in the region of T'ai-ts'ang, and the second "on a fortunate day in the second winter month between 5th December 1431 and 3rd January 1432" at Ch'ang-lo in Fukien):

1. The *Tao-ichih-lüeh* of Wang Ta-yuan, dated 1349.
2. The *Ying-yai sheng-lan* of Ma Huan, dated between 1425 and 1432 (?).
3. The *Hsing-ch'a sheng-lan* of Fei Hsin, of 1436.
4. *The Hsi-yang ch'ao-king tien-lu* of Huang Sheng-ts'eng, which appeared in 1520.[121]

In the *Tao-i chih-lüeh* one finds, *inter alia*, descriptions (not very dissimilar in presentation and substance from those contained in earlier or later chronicles) of the localities of Ts'eng-yao-lo (? Zanguebar or Zanzibar), Kan-ma-li (? Comoro islands) and Li-ch'ien-t'a and Lo-p'o-ssu (both on the Berbera coast). Of these desert lands in the Horn of Africa and of its populations leading a life of frequent hardship in a torrid climate the Chinese must have taken away a vivid impression, to judge by the striking reflections with which the author of the *Tao-i chih-lüeh* concludes his narrative: "What are the differences in climate a thousand *li* to the north and south of the Lo (river) compared to those of the miserable countries in the Ocean! This country is scorching hot, so the inhabitants need not be concerned at not having any clothing, and they naturally follow the moving chariot of space and time. No wonder they gobble their food, that they do not choose their nesting places, and that they are not concerned with trade; it is the Paradise of remote antiquity!"[122]

In the preface to the *Ying-yai sheng-lan* of Ma Huan one reads that in the year 1413 the Emperor Yung-lo (1403–24) ordered the eunuch Cheng Ho to take ships and sail to explore the foreign peoples of the West. Ma Huan writes: "I had bestowed on me by the Throne the post of interpreter of foreign languages and writing to the mission. After having voyaged endless thousand and myriads of *li* across the boundless waving waters of the Ocean, and after having seen the different states, their varying seasons and climates, their peoples and their products, I came to know that not only were the statements of the *T'ao-i chih*[123] concerning foreign lands not lies, but that there were even more wonderful and stranger things than it had told of. So I have . . . come to compose this book which I have called Ying-yai sheng-lan, or 'A comprehensive survey of the shores of the Ocean'."[124]

But it is in the *Hsing-ch'a sheng-lan* of Fei Hsin that one finds the most precise accounts and descriptions of the coasts of Africa, and in particular the coastal centres of the present Somalia, and it is for the most part these descriptions that have been taken up, albeit summarily, in the writings of Davidson, Pirone and Girace.[125]

Fei Hsin's work is divided into four chapters: the first treats of Java and the South-East Asian archipelago, the second of Ceylon and the Maldive islands, the third of the coasts of India, and the fourth of Hormuz and the coasts of Arabia and Africa. It is in this fourth chapter that one reads the extraordinarily vivid and graphic descriptions of these localities and of the peoples who dwelt on the Somali shores of the Indian Ocean. The cities are, according to their order in the *Hsing-ch'a sheng-lan*, Pu-la-wa (Brava), Chu-pu (Giumbo), and Mu-ku-tu-shu (Mogadishu). Also mentioned is the city of La-sa, which some writers would identify with Zeila.[126]

Fei Hsin writes of Brava (Pu-la-wa): "Going south from Pieh-(li)-lo [Belligam] in Msi-lan [Ceylon] one can reach this country in twenty-one days. It is near the country of Mu-ku-tu-shu [Mogadishu] and lies along the sea-coast. The town walls are made of rocks, the houses of layers of stones. The island is without vegetation, the land a broad, salty waste. It has a salt lake in which, however, grow trees with branches. After a long time they pull them out of the water, when their fruits, or seeds, become white salt. In their habits the people are virtuous. They do not till the soil, but earn their living by fishing. Men and women roll up their hair, wear a short shirt, and wrap around them a piece of cotton. The women wear gold coins in their ears, and around their necks a pendant fringe. They have only onions and garlic, but no gourds of any kind. The natural products are the *ma-ha* animal (civet cat?) which is like the *shê-chang* (musk deer), the *hua-fu-lu* (zebra) which is like a piebald donkey, leopards, *chi* deer, rhinoceros, myrrh, frankincense, ambergris, elephants' tusks, and camels. The goods used [by the Chinese] in trading are gold, silver, satins, silks, rice, beans, and china-ware. The ruler, touched by the imperial bounty, sent tributes to our Court."[127]

Of Giumbo (Chu-pu) Fei Hsin writes: "This locality is adjacent to Mu-ku-tu-shu [Mogadishu]. The village is pretty deserted. The walls are of rocks, the houses of layers of stones. Here also the customs are pure. Men and women roll up their hair. The men wrap around them a piece of cotton cloth; the women, when they go out, have a head-covering of cotton cloth; they do not expose either their bodies or their faces. The soil is of a yellowish, reddish colour. For a number of years it may not rain. There is no vegetation. They draw water with cog-wheels from deep wells. They earn their living by fishing. The natural products are lions, gold coins, leopards, camel-footed birds [ostriches], which are six or seven feet tall, frankincense, amber. The goods used [by the Chinese] in trading are vermilion (?), satins, light silks, gold, silver, china-ware, pepper, rice. The ruler, having received the imperial presents, was filled with gratitude, and sent articles of tribute."[128]

The following is Fei Hsin's description of Mogadishu (Mu-ku-tu-shu): "Going from Ksiao Ko-lan [Kulam] with a favourable wind one can reach this country in twenty days. It is on the sea-coast. The walls are piles of stones, the houses are of layers of stones and four or five storeys high, the cooking and the entertaining of guests all being done on top. The men do up their hair in knots hanging all around and wrap cotton cloth around their waists. The women do up their hair in a chignon behind and brighten up the crown with yellow varnish. From their ears hang a number of strings [of coins?], around their necks they wear silver rings, and a fringe hangs down on the breast. When they go out, they cover themselves with a cotton sheet, and veil their faces with blue gauze. On their feet they wear shoes or leather slippers. Near the [foot of the] mountain the country is a desert of brownish soil and stones. The soil is poor, the crops sparse. It may not rain [sometimes] for a number of years. They make very deep wells and draw up the water in sheep-skin bags by means of cog-wheels. They are excitable and obstinate. Archery is a part of their military training. The rich are neighbourly with the people. The poor people get their living by catching sea-fish in nets; these they dry and eat, and also feed their camels, horses, cattle and sheep on them. The native products are frankincense, gold coins, leopards, ambergris. The goods used in trading [here by the Chinese] are gold, silver, coloured satins, sandal-wood, rice, china-ware, coloured taffetas. The ruler, in pursuance of custom, brought articles of tribute."[129]

"From these accounts", Girace writes, "it is easy to see that the futa and the garbassar were already in use 450 years ago. As for the mountains, it is clear that the term refers to the almost unbroken line of coastal dunes which, especially between Merca and Brava, have a red colouring."[130]

Fei Hsin prepared two different editions of his work, one consisting of pure and simple descriptions of the countries visited, and the other being a book of illustrations presented to the Emperor to win his good graces.[131]

In the translation of the Chinese texts made by Duyvendak under the care of Youssouf Kamal,[132] Fei Hsin's book or travel journal is presented (a) in the version T'ien-yi-ko, with preface of 1436, and (b) in the usual edition revised in 1450. The order in which the African coastal centres are presented is not identical in the two versions; among the non-African coastal centres both include that of La-sa, and the 1450 edition also contains the description of A-tan (Aden). There are no appreciable differences in the editing of the two texts, and they only differ in a few details from Rockhill and Hirth's translation. For example, the usual revised edition of 1450, as translated by Duyvendak, gives the following description of Mogadishu: "The mountains are unbroken and the land is desert. The stony ground is of a yellowish-red colour; the fields are dried up and little can be gathered from them. It does not rain for years on end. The people dig very deep wells, and, with the aid of a toothed wheel, draw up water in sheepskin buckets. By nature they are quarrelsome and obstinate. As a military exercise they practise shooting with the bow. The rich people turn to seafaring and trading with distant places. The poor people fish with nets; they eat the fish after drying it in the sun, and also feed it to their camels, horses, oxen and sheep."[133]

The account given in the Ming History (Ming shih) of the coastal centres of Somalia, which Duyvendak translated in 1939, says that in the fourteenth year of Yung-lo's reign Mogadishu "sent an embassy and, with the countries of Brava and Malindi, presented a letter of felicitations, rendering homage to the Court and bringing tribute. Cheng Ho received the order to go there carrying an imperial decree, and silk. He left in company with ambassadors to recompense [the king of that country]. Later [the ambassadors] returned carrying tribute, and once more [the Emperor] ordered [Cheng] Ho to accompany them to present flowered silk to the King and to his concubines. In the 21st year (1423) ambassadors again appeared with tribute and, when they left, they again took away gifts for the King and his concubines. In the fifth year of Hsüan-te's reign [1430] an edict for these countries was again published."

Of Brava the Ming History says: "Between the 14th year of Yung-lo's reign [1416] and the 21st this country in all sent tribute four times, and at the same times as the expeditions to Mogadishu Cheng Ho was also sent twice as ambassador to that country." Of Giumbo the Ming History only says that "Cheng Ho visited that country".[134]

The brief descriptions which the Ming History gives of these Somali coastal areas always emphasize their desert character, aridity and poverty of resources. On the other hand it dwells at greater length on Aden, both on the cordial relations established between it and China under the first two Ming Emperors and earlier in the Liang (502–57), Sui (590–618) and T'ang (618–906) dynasties, and also on the nature of the country, presented as generally attractive in spite of the violent character of its inhabitants. "This land is fertile and there is an abundance of millet and barley. . . . The climate is always pleasant. . . . The four seasons have no fixed times. They [the inhabitants] have their own astronomers who calculate the day on which spring will begin, and in fact, the flowers begin to blossom on that day." In the richness of its fauna, it is stated, the country has no equal; and the giraffe and the lion are described in a few lively and telling phrases.[135]

What of course surprises one in this account of Aden is the favourable presentation of its climate, natural conditions and resources, which contrast sharply with Aden's actual climate and character. This difference in the visitor's impressions, compared with his impressions of the coastal centre of Somalia (where nature is certainly no harsher than in Aden), can only be explained by the supposition that the latter place was visited by the Chinese during a rainy season, and the Somali localities during the hot dry season (from December to March).

Chinese coins found in coastal areas in Somalia: reverse (*From T'oung Pao, by kind permission of Messrs. Brill of Leyden*)

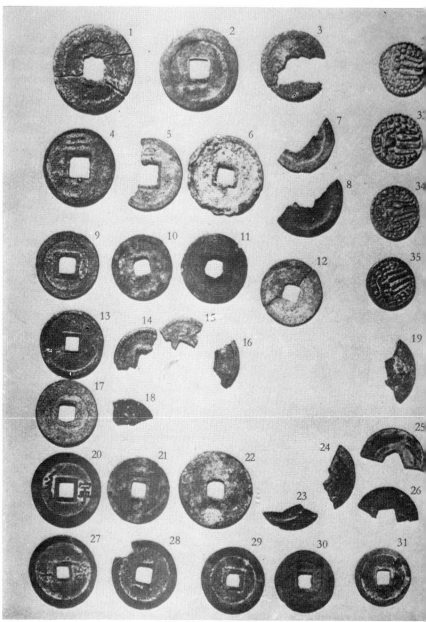

9   Chinese coins found in coastal areas of Somalia: obverse (*From T'oung Pao, b kind permission of Messrs. Brill of Leyden*)

VII

Chinese Coins and Porcelain
on the East African Coast

The finds of Chinese coins of the T'ang (AD 618–906) and Sung dynasties between Mogadishu and Zanzibar and of pottery and porcelain of the same periods, taken together with the various references in Chinese, Arab and European authors, do not seem sufficient to dispel all doubts as to whether voyages by Chinese to these shores, for commercial or diplomatic ends, were actually made before the advent of the Ming dynasty (1368–1644).

For the early Ming period—that is, when the authenticated expeditions directed by Cheng Ho between 1417 and 1433 reached the Somali shores—there remains evident testimony in the form of numerous fragments of splendid porcelain, with only rare coins. We have already referred to the motives which accounted for the abundance of the first and the scarcity of the second.

According to Ingrams, China's trade relations with the east coast of Africa probably extended over a period of four dynasties, from AD 618 to 1644. Some of the numerous coins found at Mogadishu, Kilwa and Mafia have been identified as belonging to the T'ang dynasty, to the "k'ai-yüan" period (713–41), while others are dated to 845. "It is also recorded that Abu Zeyd Hassan returned from China via East Africa some time after 851. It is obvious therefore that there was intercourse with China from an early date. Nevertheless the T'ang dynasty intercourse with the outside world was not much encouraged. During the succeeding dynasty, that of the Sungs (960–1279), there was far more intercourse."[136]

This only goes to confirm the earlier statement of Pearce: "In addition to the trade from Arabia and India, there is historical proof that the Chinese also visited the East African coast during medieval times. The intercourse between the Far East and Africa is confirmed by the find of numerous Chinese coins at Mogadishu, Kilwa, Mafia, and at other Azanian ports. A number of these coins discovered at the first-named place have been assigned dates by Dr. Friedrich Hirth of Munich as ranging from AD 845 to 1163. A Chinese coin found in 1916 at Mafia island has been examined by the Department of Coins at the British Museum, and stated to be a 'cash' of the

Emperor Shen Tsung, who reigned between AD 1068 and 1086."[137]

Ingrams also refers to the coin found at Mafia in 1916 and to other coins dated to the "shao-hsing" period.[138]

Dr. W. S. Bushell, in a review of a book by Hirth[139] which appeared in the *North China Daily News* of 9th May 1888, recalled that Sir John Kirk, while residing in Zanzibar as British Consul General, had assembled a collection of ancient Chinese celadon ware, which had later been deposited in the British Museum. Coins of the Sung dynasty had also come to light in Kirk's excavations—strong evidence of the vigorous nature of Chinese trade with the West in that period, which Kuwabara emphasizes in his study "On P'u Shou-kêng".

Hirth noted later[140] that in April 1908 two small collections of Chinese coins came into the possession of Dr. F. L. Stuhlmann and Justus Strandes. The first said that he found his collection of eight coins (with a large number of fragments of celadon ware) when excavating in the vicinity of Mogadishu; the second had obtained his collection of seven coins in the same locality. The coins, which were in a bad state of conservation, nevertheless appeared without exception to be of the Chinese type, being of bronze, round, with a square hole in the centre. They were all considered to be of earlier date than the beginning of the thirteenth century, and were mainly dated to the eleventh and twelfth centuries. Both these collections were given to the Museum für Völkerkunde in Berlin.

In recent years Freeman-Grenville has done some very fine research on the coins of East Africa, from the most remote times to the end of the nineteenth century. Of these he gave a detailed description in 1957, giving all references to previous finds, and returned to the subject in 1959 and 1960 confirming the dates and other details relevant to the Chinese coins.[141]

In a letter of 9th July 1962 from Mombasa, Professor Kirkman wrote to the author: "Chinese coins and charms are extremely rare in Kenya. I have found half a dozen in 14 years of excavation: all except one, which was early Ming, are southern Sung but they were found in late XIV century contexts. They are, however, more common in Zanzibar."

The most sensational find was in fact at Zanzibar, in 1945: a Mhadimu farmer, Makame bin Mwalimu, had the good fortune to turn up, while preparing for planting his land on the coral barrier of Kajengwa near Makunduchi (Zanzibar), a considerable cache of not less than 250 coins, all Chinese. The date of these, as of the few found earlier, excepting the unpublished collection of Mogadishu,[142] can be broadly within the wide span of years AD 618–1295, and thus they belong entirely to the T'ang and Sung dynasties.

However, of the eight coins forming the Mogadishu collection, six are of the Emperor Yung-lo (1403–24) of the Ming dynasty, one of the seventeenth century and one of the nineteenth century. Freeman-Grenville considers that the first group of coins may very well be connected with Cheng Ho's voyages.[143]

Considering the period to which these coins of the so-called Mogadishu collection have been attributed, it does not seem that they can be confused with the other collection of eight coins found by Stuhlman in the same city and dated to a much earlier period— unless, of course, there has been an error of identification.

In 1959 Professor Hulsewé, of the Sinologisch Instituut in Leyden, reported on an interesting series of Chinese coins (figs. 9 and 10) which were sent to the directing board of the journal T'oung Pao for identification.[144] Of the 32 coins (four others, nos. 32–35, are from Ceylon and dated to between 1153 and 1296) five were found at Brava, one (no. 16) near Merca and the other 25 at Mogadishu or in its vicinity.

Some of these coins were whole, one had only a fragment missing, and 13 (nos. 3, 5, 7, 8, 14, 15, 16, 18, 19, 23, 24, 25, 26) consisted only of fragments of various sizes. They were dated as follows: no. 1 to the Nan T'ang dynasty (934–61), nos. 17 and 18 to the Ming dynasty and in fact to the reign of the Emperor Yung-lo (1403–24), and nos. 2–16 to the Sung period (1017–1252). The rest (nos. 19–31) were either of more recent date or were too fragmentary to be datable.

Professor Hulsewé stated: "The coins are too few in number to permit of any statistical conclusions; apart from this, the fact that they are in great part ancient (Sung dynasty) is only vague evidence that they were brought to Somalia in the period to which they appear to belong, since old coins often remained in circulation for a long time." This supposition has also been put forward by other writers, as for example Schwarz.[145] The field of Chinese pottery and porcelain finds offers a fairly extensive range of items, many of them of undistinguished type, but others of excellent workmanship. The subject has given rise to an interesting literature, and raises problems of considerable importance.

Reference has already been made to the only superficially surprising causes of the abundance of coins of the T'ang and Sung dynasties and the scarcity of coins of the Ming dynasty. In contrast to this picture in the numismatic field, however, one encounters a complete absence of pottery and porcelain of the T'ang dynasty and preceding periods, and a considerable amount belonging to the Sung and above all the Ming dynasty.

In 1920 Pearce wrote that much Chinese porcelain or porcelain fragments found in the ancient inhabited centres of the island of

Pemba, such as Ndagoni and Mtambwe, had been examined and classified chronologically by the Department of Ceramics of the Victoria and Albert Museum. Some of these finds belong to more recent periods (seventeenth and eighteenth centuries) but a number belong to periods synchronous with the contacts established in medieval times between China and the coasts or islands of East Africa. They include:

(*a*) a bowl in fragments, cream-coloured Ting ware, Sung dynasty (960–1279)

(*b*) two fragments of rims of dishes, dark grey stone ware, brownish celadon glaze, Sung or Ming dynasty

(*c*) fragment of a base of a bowl, incised ornament, greyish celadon glaze, Sung dynasty

(*d*) fragment of a base of a bowl, greyish celadon, Sung dynasty

(*e*) base of a bowl, impressed fish, celadon glaze, Ming dynasty

(*f*) two fragments of fluted dishes, celadon glaze, Ming dynasty

(*g*) fragment of bowl, relief ornament inside, celadon glaze, Ming dynasty

(*h*) five fragments of vessels, celadon glaze, Ming dynasty

(*i*) three fragments, cream-coloured Ting ware, probably Sung dynasty.[146]

Pearce says that he himself recovered from an ancient tomb on Pemba island a bowl which the Department of Ceramics of the Victoria and Albert Museum classified as cream-coloured Ming porcelain of the Sung dynasty.[147]

Finds of Chinese vessels of the type discovered at Pemba have been made all along the East African coast and at Zimbabwe itself.[148] The variety of workmanship and typology seems fairly wide; and from the quantity which turns up on beaches and among ruins one can conclude that the importation of Chinese porcelain in East Africa during the Middle Ages was carried out on a large scale.[149]

Some decades before Pearce, Strandes saw "in the porcelain fragments found everywhere among ancient ruins in East Africa, classifiable by experts as belonging to the famous celadon porcelain, a further proof of the relations which existed so long ago between China and East Africa".[150] Stuhlmann, on the same subject, affirmed without a shadow of doubt that the plates and bowls of celadon porcelain used in ancient times to decorate tombs in East Africa had been brought directly from China.[151]

Tanner, referring to Chinese pottery found on the island of Kilwa Kisiwani in 1948–49, observes that the Chinese carried on a considerable export traffic with the countries of western Asia and Africa, which reached its peak about half way through the sixteenth century and continued with less intensity after the Portuguese conquest. Items of blue-and-white and green ware have in fact been found, he notes, all along the coast of eastern Africa as far as the Cape of Good Hope, where some fragments were found in the wreck of a Dutch ship. With few exceptions, these were of little note as regards workmanship and design, catering for a market which continued to take products now out of fashion in China itself; so that finds of indisputable Sung characteristics could in fact belong to a period later than that dynasty.[152]

Tanner is of the opinion that the greater part of this Sung-type ware belongs to the first half of the Ming period, since it has a white body under the glaze, whereas the typical Lung-chuen celadon has a grey body.

Yet this attribution of Ming date to Sung-type ware would seem somewhat hazardous, not least because about a century intervened between the end of the Sung dynasty and the beginning of the Ming dynasty, this being the period covered by the Mongol Yüan dynasty (1280–1367). However this may be, Tanner himself very prudently adds that with Chinese ceramics no question is more controversial than that of establishing which is Ming and which Sung.

One is also not fully prepared to follow Tanner in his interpretation of the fact that "although the pottery is thought to be all of a date later than the sixteenth century a series of coins collected from the same site at the same time were predominantly of a slightly earlier date than the earliest Chinese pottery". Apart from the consideration adduced by Professor Hulsewé, that coins generally remained in circulation for a long time and thus were of dates earlier than the time when they were actually brought to the African coasts, there are in fact very many finds to which dates much earlier than the fifteenth century have been assigned.

Freeman-Grenville writes: "In days long gone by there was a considerable import trade in Chinese porcelain in East Africa. There are small collections of it in the Dar-es-Salaam Museum, in the Beit al-Amani at Zanzibar, in the collection of the late Sir Frederick Jackson in the Uganda Museum, as well as some in private hands.[153] In the past two years my wife and I have assembled a collection of some 400 shards from more than 30 ancient sites between the Kenya border and the Rufiji. From all these shards it is now beginning to be possible to reconstruct a history of this trade for which we have virtually no written evidence but only that of the pots themselves.

"We know that in 1417 and 1431 Chinese embassies visited Mogadishu and Malindi; but, apart from these occasions it is concluded by G. F. Hourani, whose 'Arab Seafarers in the Indian Ocean' everyone interested in East African history ought to read, that trade between the East Coast and China was entirely conducted through entrepots, without direct contact. . . .

"Although there is evidence for the import of Sung celadon wares, it seems that heavy imports of Chinese wares started quite suddenly about the middle of the 14th century. Failing to obtain good class Middle Eastern earthenware, the Arab importers turned to India and started to buy Chinese wares in the markets there. Indeed, apart from finds at Gedi, although some doubtful Sung ware has been found at Tongoni, and a single fragment of Ting ware in Zanzibar, we can say that before the mid-14th century there was probably no steady import of Chinese ware.

"From then on, there is hardly a single reign of a Chinese Emperor not represented in finds of porcelain on the Tanganyika coast up to the mid-19th century. But probably because there has been no systematic excavation, examples of the early Ming of the 14th and 15th centuries are rare."[154]

The porcelain was mainly destined for domestic use, and was utilitarian rather than precious. But it was also employed for decoration of public and private buildings, and especially of tombs— a usage perhaps introduced from India. "Only two mosques in East Africa retain their decoration of porcelain plates round the *mihrab* or prayer niche: Chwaka in Zanzibar and Mafia, a remote place in Pangani District. . . . Far more familiar are the tombs decorated with Chinese porcelain which may be found at almost every historical site. The earliest known of these, which has recently been the subject of a study in *Tanganyika Notes and Records*, by Mr. Graham Hunter, is a pillar tomb at Kauli, near Bagamoyo; it was decorated with plates of the Yuan dynasty (1272–1368), of which the two last remaining have now been most wisely removed to the safe custody of the King George V Memorial Museum."[155]

The decoration of tombs and mosques by fixing plates and bowls to the walls must be considered typical of Shirazi or Persian cult usage.[156]

The Coryndon Museum in Nairobi has a small but rare collection of Chinese ware, in a good state of preservation. It comprises, in particular, a large salad bowl; a large plate; two small bowls, one of paler and the other of darker colour; and a large black enamel vase. These pieces appeared not to have been identified or exactly dated, and in response to my request the Museum in June 1962 kindly invited Professor Kirkman to express an opinion on them. He said that this porcelain, all celadon, had come to light after a landslip at Ngomeni, 18 miles north of Malindi, in 1929. In his opinion the items could be dated as follows: the large salad bowl to the fourteenth century; the large plate to the fourteenth or fifteenth century; and the two small bowls to the fourteenth and fifteenth centuries respectively. The large vase had been unearthed at Kisarini and given by Sheikh Ali bin Salim to Mr. Tate in 1922. It was dated by Professor Kirkman to a later period (sixteenth or seventeenth century).

The fact that whole Chinese porcelain objects are only rarely found can be attributed, in general, to the ravages of time, to the successive waves of conquest and sacking which these localities have suffered, to the neglect to which monuments, tombs and dwellings were abandoned in the past, and perhaps to the actual fragility of the material. However, one should not overlook another suggestive circumstance, noted by Freeman-Grenville: in the Book of the District of Pangani in Tanganyika a writer relates that at the funeral of Zumbe Diwani Simba of Mkwaja in 1911 porcelain plates were broken, as a ritual act, over the tomb of the dead man.[157]

One may also instance, as relevant to the general subject, the series of porcelain objects cited and in part discovered by Pearce in the tombs situated to the west of the great mosque of Mkumbuu on the island of Pemba and those found in the nearby houses (the house on the beach and the House of the Tombs).

This porcelain, presented and described by Kirkman, was found at different levels, indicating different periods; the oldest comprised pieces perhaps datable to the thirteenth century, and the less old probably datable to the beginning of the fifteenth century.[158]

Kirkman states: "The dating of the early levels at Mkumbuu, as at all sites, offers great difficulties. In view of the homogeneity of the ceramic, I am reluctant, perhaps unduly, to concede a period of as much as two hundred years—that is, AD 1200 to AD 1400—in which there was apparently no change in fashion in local earthenware, Islamic glazed ware and Chinese porcelain." However, the amount of Chinese porcelain found in the Ras Mkumbuu excavations is less than that found at Gedi and Kilepwa.[159]

Kirkman also presented detailed accounts, at the end of 1956 and the beginning of 1957, of excavations conducted from 1948 to 1956 in some ancient cities in Kenya.[160]

The East African coast, from Mogadishu to the Mozambique borders, with the islands of Zanzibar, Pemba, Mafia and other smaller islands, was until 1948 among the most interesting but also the least known areas from the archaeological standpoint. Neither Britain nor Germany nor Italy, the nations responsible for the colonial administration of these territories, had been at any pains to seek among the ruins and the monuments the traces of a largely hidden past.

In 1948 the archaeological zone of the city of Gedi, 65 miles north of Mombasa and 10 miles south of Malindi, was decleared a protected area and entrusted to the care of a Warden. In March 1948 excavations began and were later extended to various other localities in Kenya, from the Lamu archipelago in the north to the island of Mombasa in the south. The most extensive and important of these digs were at Ungwana, near the outlet of the Tana river, where in an area of about 45 acres—about the size of the Gedi site—there were still standing six ancient mosques and a number of large houses and decorated tombs. Excavations were also carried out at Kilepwa, Mnarani, Takwa (on Manda island, opposite Lamu), Malindi, Kinuni, and the Mosque of the Three Tribes on the island of Mombasa.

In an article published in December 1956 Kirkman pointed out: "The important northern area between the Lamu archipelago and Somalia, the apparently less important area south of Mombasa, and the important towns of Mombasa, Lamu and Malindi still remain uninvestigated."[161] Of the eight zones excavated, in three, at Gedi, Ungwana and Kilepwa, the most ancient material found had exhibited the same characteristics, being datable to the thirteenth and perhaps even to the twelfth century. The oldest finds at Mnarani, on the other hand, were datable to the fourteenth century, and the tomb pillars at Malindi, Takwa and Kinuni to the fifteenth century.

The quantity of celadon fragments brought to light in these excavations was very considerable, although whole specimens were fairly few in number. Contrary to earlier assertions, in the opinion of Kirkman himself all this material is to be assigned not to the Sung period but to the early Ming and in some case the Yüan. "Chinese porcelain and stoneware were reaching the Near East in gradually increasing quantities from the ninth or tenth centuries; but there is no evidence that it reached East Africa until much later, when the Sung dynasty was a thing of the past. . . . Variations of tint and glaze apparently mean very little in distinguishing between the 14th and 15th centuries."[162]

Among the ruined courtyards of the houses and the mosques and inside or near the tombs were found fragments of antique Ming porcelain with painted borders and representations of birds and stags. From these finds one can deduce that in about the middle of the fourteenth century the brown and white celadon ware became more common, giving rise in its turn to the adoption of new shapes and styles of ornament in the local pottery.

The fifteenth century was the golden age for these coastal cities of East Africa, and many of their buildings that are worthy of archaeological study belong to this period. During this century there was also a notable increase in trade with overseas countries, from the

10 Chinese vase with dragons in grey-blue on a grey ground, mid-14th century, found by Kirkman at Kilepwa in 1948

11   Late Ming blue-and-white plate found near the Mosque at Gedi

12 Copper-red vase found in the upper level by the Great Mosque of Gedi

13　Celadon plate found at Gedi

14　Ming blue-and-white porcelain plate found set into a tomb pillar at Mambrui

Near to the Far East. Celadon porcelain was then imported in large quantities, and with it lesser quantities of *ying ch'ing*, white porcelain, and brown stoneware. The blue-and-white ware was found in levels corresponding to the beginning of the fifteenth century (becoming more common towards the end of the century); but celadon remained the principal Chinese porcelain until the sixteenth century.[163]

Kirkman has also published a meticulous and revealing account of the excavations carried out from 1948 among the the ruins of the mosque, the tomb pillars and the dwelling houses of the small island of Kilepwa, 50 miles north of Mombasa and two miles south of Gedi. Here also there were numerous finds of porcelain of Far Eastern provenance, and celadon was present in all levels except the first. Lead-glazed stoneware was found in all levels except the first, while the blue-and-white porcelain found belonged only to the most recent phase. In particular the best preserved and earliest of the objects found were discovered in the tombs, as in the case of the tomb pillars of Malindi;[164] among the most important finds were some bowls of greenish white and clear grey, and a bottle or vase with designs of dragons in grey-blue on a grey ground, datable to the middle of the fourteenth century (fig. 10).

Excavations a few years later, described by Kirkman with his customary scientific precision, were carried out at Kilifi, the present Mnarani, on the south side of a creek 35 miles north of Mombasa, which was part of the old city state of Kilifi. Here are the remains of two mosques, the foundations of a third and a group of tombs with decorations of incised coral and Arabic inscriptions. Among the finds at various levels the celadon fragments and Chinese vessels datable to the fourteenth and fifteenth centuries were so numerous that, as Kirkman says, if prosperity were to be measured by the quantity of Chinese imports, the fifteenth century must have been the most flourishing period of Kilifi and perhaps of other cities in this region.[165]

Equally important and interesting finds, also due to Kirkman, came from the excavations carried out at Gedi by the Royal National Parks of Kenya. These brought to light an Arab tomb with the date of AH 802 (1399); the objects of porcelain and Chinese stoneware found beneath and above the pavement of the tomb, as is apparent from Kirkman's descriptions and drawings, had certain notable features in common.[166]

Other authentic evidence comes from Mathew's accounts of the results of excavations in the archaeological zone of the islands of the Kilwa group, and in particular the island of Mnara which offers two interesting groups of ruins (Site A and Site B). In the first have been found fragments of porcelain classified as Yüan or late Sung, and a series of fragments of the early and middle Ming period, among which blue-and-white was slightly more numerous than celadon.[167]

In the "Arab Fort" of Jereza, on the island of Kilwa Kisiwani, numerous fragments of Chinese pottery were found in the entrance passage, all however datable to the sixteenth century or later. A sole fragment of celadon was found among the detritus of the rooms at the south-west end of the building, which had been repaired at various times; this find was of considerable interest, consisting of the base of a large celadon vase of good workmanship, probably Lung-chuan ware of the fourteenth or fifteenth century.[168]

The excavations carried out by the Department of Antiquities of Tanganyika in many localities have not infrequently brought to light more or less important items of Chinese porcelain, some of earlier date than the sixteenth century. In Kaole, for example, numerous celadon fragments datable to the fifteenth century were found;[169] remains of a Chinese cylindrical vase were found in the Well of Husuni Ndogo at Kilwa[170] and remains of Chinese blue-and-white porcelain and celadon (datable in large part to the fifteenth century) in the Great Mosque of Kilwa and at Nguruni and Kera.[171]

These brief notes are only intended to give a general idea of the vastness and the interest of this field of research, which yields such clear evidence of the extent of direct and indirect traffic between China and the coasts of East Africa during the last centuries of the Middle Ages.

The subject is now well charted—although with many gaps—thanks to the perceptive explorations of a series of scholars, from the end of the nineteenth century until today, aided by increasingly rigorous archaeological research. Pioneers in the field were Bretschneider,[172] Strandes, Pearce, Hirth and Chavannes. More recently, the dedicated exertions of men like Gray, Kirkman, Robinson, Freeman-Grenville, Fripp, Mathew, Pope, Tanner, Hunter, Chittick and others, for English-speaking Africa, have made very substantial contributions to the subject.

As regards finds of pottery and porcelain on the Somali coasts and in the Gulf of Aden, interesting evidence came to light with Curle's excavations of 1934 among the four groups of ancient ruined cities discovered in the hinterland of the former British Somaliland. These centres, situated on an almost unbroken ridge extending from behind Zeila to behind Berbera, seem to have been particularly flourishing between the fifteenth and sixteenth centuries. This is evident from elements of their buildings and from mounds in or near these. Celadon fragments were far from rare, including some large enough to be identified as belonging to Sung and Ming dynasties, between the twelfth and fifteenth centuries. Other blue-

and-white porcelain fragments were datable to the seventeenth century.[173]

Later Grottanelli, on an expedition to the Bajun islands, was able to find and classify various fragments of porcelain collected at Giula, Ngumi, Ciovayi and Rasini. At least eight of these are datable to the Ming dynasty.[174]

All these findings and researches ought to be collated so as to form a composite picture of the essential basis of the subject. This should be supplemented by precise details and identifications of the pieces belonging to both African and non-African museums, and if possible also details of private collections.[175]

This not inconsiderable accumulation of data may of course be enriched, and perhaps given a new aspect, by systematic excavation which may be promoted by appropriate bodies in English-speaking East Africa in areas not yet investigated, from the Tana river to the Usambara plateau and from the Dar es Salaam area to the district of Inyanga in Rhodesia.[176] Excavation could also be rewarding along the coast of Mozambique, and above all along the coast of Somalia and in particular in the area near the present airfield of Mogadishu (where there has recently been a good deal of building), known in history under the name of Hamar Gaġġab, "shattered Mogadishu".[177] This latter area should yield some interesting surprises, if it is still the case that, after the spring rains, with the water boring down into the sand of the dunes, coins get carried to the surface of the sloping ground.[178]

VIII

The Dates of the Early Ming Voyages to the West

Cheng Ho—as Pelliot noted in 1933[179]—had had a number of commemorative inscriptions cut, and one of these, in three languages, was found in Ceylon in about 1913.[180] But when Pelliot was writing, Cheng Ho's other two inscriptions had not yet been discovered. They were to form the basis of Duyvendak's study, "The true dates of the Chinese maritime expeditions in the early fifteenth century".

Pelliot, however, had been able to establish—unlike the Sinologists who preceded him in the exploration of this interesting chapter of Chinese maritime and commercial expansion—that some documents should not be regarded as original, and that, for example, Rockhill in examining the *Ying-yai sheng-lan* had very probably taken the recasting for the original, thus attributing the original to Chang Sheng who had done the recasting.[181]

In his detailed exegesis Pelliot tries to establish with certainty the dates and the destinations of the seven voyages of Cheng Ho—which Duyvendak was later to correct on the evidence of the two inscriptions found and deciphered between 1935 and 1937.

Of the first expedition Pelliot tells us: "In the third year of the Emperor Yung-lo, in the sixth moon (27th June–25th July 1405) the order was given to [Cheng Ho] and his colleagues Wang Ching-hung and others to set forth on an embassy to the western seas. They took more than 27,800 men, comprising officers and soldiers, took on board an abundance of gifts of gold and silks, and built for the purpose 62 ocean-going junks 440 feet long and 180 feet wide."[182] After passing familiar and friendly lands they visited "various barbarian kingdoms where they published the edicts of the Son of Heaven. On such occasions they presented gifts to the princes and chiefs of these countries; those who did not submit were brought to reason by military [force]. On the fifth year of Yung-lo, in the ninth moon (1st–30th October 1407), they returned home."[183]

It is certain that on this first expedition Cheng Ho's fleet cannot have got much further than India. The second expedition left China in the sixth year of Yung-lo, in the ninth moon (20th September–

18th October 1408), returning in the ninth year in the sixth moon, on 6th July 1411. The third left China in the tenth year of Yung-lo in the eleventh moon (4th December–2nd January 1413), returning in the thirteenth year in the seventh moon, on 12th August 1415. Neither of these voyages took the fleet beyond Ceylon; they probably amounted, like the first, to different kinds of punitive expeditions against pirates or kings who did not submit to the behests of the conqueror.

The fourth voyage was undoubtedly the longest, and is for us the most interesting, both for its apparent motives and for the objects it achieved. In the fourteenth year of Yung-lo in the winter (that is, between 21st October and 17th January 1417) 19 kingdoms, including those of Malaya and Calicut, sent embassies to bear gifts and tribute to Court. In the principal Annals of 1416 the list of the countries visited in the course of this expedition is incomplete; but chapter 326 of the *Ming-shih* relates that Cheng Ho went to Mu-ku-tu-shu (Mogedoxu or Mogadishu), Pu-la-wa (Brawa or Brava) and La-sa (? Zeila). These are the three countries that are stated to have sent embassies in 1416, as well as the country of Ma-lin (Malindi), but the latter is not mentioned, perhaps through oversight, in this chapter 326 of the *Ming-shih* (while it figures in the biography of Cheng Ho among the countries which he in fact visited). Indeed, it was Ma-lin which a year before, as has been noted, had sent an embassy with the gift of a giraffe or *ch'i-lin*, whose arrival had produced such a sensation at Court.[184]

"The four states, or at least three of them", writes Pelliot, "are on the east coast of Africa, and Ma-lin must be Malindi, north of Mombasa, as Rockhill thinks, especially since the map in the *Wu-pei-chih* gives it as Ma-lin-ti. La-sa is not identifiable; in Rockhill's view it could be some port near Ma-lin, or with a transposition of syllables (La-sa = Sa-la) might be the town of Zeila in the former British Somaliland; but neither supposition appears confirmed by any other evidence that we have to hand."[185]

The fourth voyage was begun in the spring of the nineteenth year of Yung-lo (i.e. between 2nd February and 1st May 1421) and in this case also the chronicle relates that Cheng Ho after India went on to the coasts of Arabia at Jufar and the east coast of Africa at Mogadishu and Brava (the other ports of call are not indicated). In the eighth moon (17th August–15th September 1422) the fleet returned to the Chinese harbours.

In the twenty-second year of Yung-lo, in the first moon (1st–29th February 1424) Cheng Ho was again sent to distant countries with the mission, *inter alia*, of taking a decree of nomination with the imperial seal to Palembang; but by the time he returned the Emperor had died.[186] So ended the series of great voyages known as the expeditions of the *pao-ch'uan* or jewel ships, since one of their aims was to bring back gems and precious objects for the Court. In fact, as Pelliot states, these large-scale expeditions had the dual aims of prestige (impressing remote foreign countries with the Emperor's authority, and conveying decrees and seals of nomination) and trade, including the acquisition of luxury goods and the jewels so much sought by the Imperial Palace.[187]

Cheng Ho's biography says that "innumerable unnamed precious objects were brought back, but at the same time the expenses borne by China were not inconsiderable." For this reason, which was exploited by the school of Court officials averse to the policy of maritime expansion and trading contracts, Yung-lo's successor Hung-hsi took the decision, on the very day of his accession (7th September 1424), to abolish many of the ventures and undertakings sponsored by his father, and among them in particular the so-called "voyages of the jewel ships".

"On that day", the principal Annals relate,[188] "were suppressed the [voyages of the] ships of the precious jewels to the western seas." And even if susequently the Emperor Hsüan-tê, who succeeded Hung-hsi very soon after, "thought fit to send embassies once, he too later renounced the enterprise".

To Hsüan-tê, in fact, is due the seventh and last voyage of Cheng Ho. It was organized in the fifth year of his reign, for motives indicated by the Emperor himself in the edict reported in the *Shih-lu* of Hsüan-tê: "I have already proclaimed a general amnesty throughout the universe and I have given to my reign the name of Hsüan-tê. All have felt themselves restored by it. But the barbarian realms, situated afar beyond the seas, still know nothing of it. I now expressly send the grand eunuchs Cheng Ho, Wang Ching-hung and others that, bearing the Imperial orders, they may go and make it known. Let each one [of these barbarian sovereigns] follow obediently the heavenly way and guide the people so that all together may enjoy the felicity of the great peace."[189]

Thus in the fifth year of Hsüan-tê, in the sixth moon (20th June–19th July 1430) Cheng Ho and Wang Ching-hung again received the order to cross the seas to Hormuz and other countries, seventeen in all; and then they returned.[190] In this expedition the authors of three of the works previously cited took part:[191] Ma Huan, author of the *Ying-yai sheng-lan*, Fei Hsin, author of the *Hsing-ch'a cheng-lan*, which contains the descriptions of the Somali coastal places already noted, and Kung Sheng, author of the *Si-yang fan-kou chih*. The total complement of this expedition amounted to 27,550, comprising officers, other ranks, helmsmen, pilots, interpreters, secretaries, book-keepers, physicians, anchormen, caulkers, carpenters, seamen and others.[192]

It is not possible to establish whether this last expedition reached the harbours of the East African coast. Fei Hsin only says that in 1432 the fleet was in Java, and then in the Nicobar islands; that a part of the gifts was sent to Calicut and to Mecca; and that, by 1432, many other countries had been visited (seventeen according to the biography of Cheng Ho, twenty according to that of Kung Sheng); the names of countries beyond Hormuz, such as Aden, Jufar, Jobo, Mogadishu and Brava, which were not explicitly mentioned, might be regarded as comprised in Feng Ho's statement, on the fleet's routes, that it "sailed directly to the realms of Hormuz *and others*".

However, the account given in chapters 325 and 326 of the *Mingshih* has Cheng Ho going also to Mo-ku-tu-shu (Mogadishu), Pu-la-wa (Brava) and La-sa (? Zeila).[193]

IX

Cheng Ho's Two Inscriptions

Cheng Ho's two inscriptions were discovered and published only in 1935–37. The text of the first, no longer extant, had become known from a writing published in *Kuo-feng* (vol. VII, no. 4 of 1st November 1935) over the signature of Cheng Hao-sheng, with the date of 2nd October 1935. The inscription had been erected by Cheng Ho in the temple of T'ien Fei, the Celestial Spouse, at Liu-chia-chiang, in the district of T'ai-ts'ang, on 14th March 1431.

The second inscription was found, also in 1935, by an official named Wang Po-ch'iu, who published a communication on the subject in January 1937. A photograph and an edition of the text were subsequently published by Chin Yün-ming in the *Journal of the Fukien Christian University* (vol. XXVI, 15th December 1937). The inscription was discovered in Ch'ang-lo in Fukien province, to which it had earlier been removed from the temple of T'ien Fei, the Celestial Spouse, everywhere venerated (fig. 7). The stone tablet itself gave the information that it had been erected by Cheng Ho and his travelling companions "on a fortunate day in the second winter moon of the year *hsin-hai*, in the sixth year of Hsüan-tê (5th December 1431–2nd January 1432).[194]

Thus ten months would have passed between the date of the first inscription and that of the second. This is easily explainable. Liu-chia-chang, the place of the first inscription, was the port near the Yang-tse estuary where the fleets assembled for the expeditions and waited while all the preparations required by such long and adventurous voyages were being made. Ch'ang-lo was the port to which the fleets transferred to wait for a favourable wind for setting out, and where the necessary provisioning was attended to.

Thus, in fact, Cheng Ho's seventh and last expedition set out from Ch'ang-lo only at the beginning of 1432, probably in January or February. Since both inscriptions were set up before setting sail for the western seas, they cannot of course give us any indication of the route of this voyage or its vicissitudes.

However, the two inscriptions of Liu-chia-chiang and Ch'ang-lo, brilliantly edited and commentated by Duyvendak in his critical

15 Section of the Wu-pei-chih map showing the East African coasts visited by Cheng Ho, first published by M. G. Phillips in 1885 (For the names assignable to Africa, see reference 195)

study of 1938, clear up many of the misunderstanding and disputes, above all as to routes and dates. previously encountered in the writings of the most noted Sinologists, who had not had the advantage of the first-hand testimony of the architect and protagonist of these bold enterprises.

One should also note that the texts which refer directly to the Chinese voyages to the West were not accompanied by maps. However, such voyages furnished the material for a sea map, contained in the work of Mau Yung-i mentioned above, *Wu-pei-chih*. "Documents on military preparations" (fig. 15). The introduction to this work, which has a date of 1621, states expressly: "The distance, countries, etc. indicated on the map have been established with meticulous exactness, to serve as an example to posterity and as a record of the military enterprises of Cheng Ho." The remark is clearly intended in appreciation of the ventures of the grand eunuch, which the new policy of Yung-lo's successors had endeavoured to consign to complete oblivion.[195]

The two inscriptions of Cheng Ho, it should be pointed out at the outset, seem to be copies, as if their author had had them cut from a single text, with differing introductions and conclusions of a mainly eulogistic or religious character.

First Inscription

Inscription on stone in the palace of the Celestial Spouse at Liu-chia-chian in eastern Lü in memory of the intercourse with the barbarians.

In the sixth year of Hsüan-tê of the Ming dynasty (1431), the cyclical year *hsin-hai*, the first day of (the second) spring (month) (March 14th), the principal envoys, the Grand Eunuchs Cheng Ho and Wang Ching-hung, the assistant-envoys, the Grand Eunuchs Chu Liang, Chou Fu, Hung Pao and Yang Chen, and the Senior

E

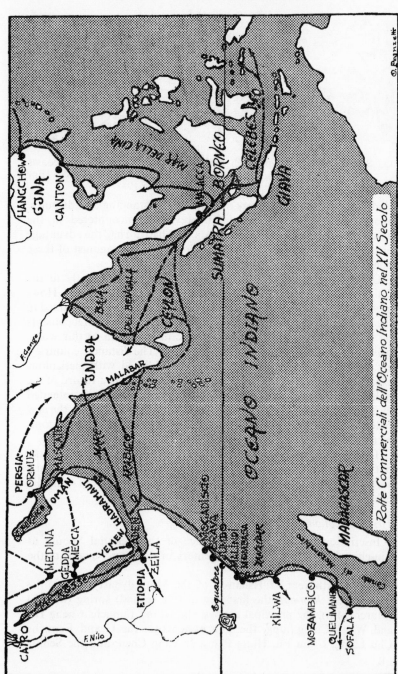

16 Indian Ocean trade routes in the fifteenth century

Lesser Eunuch Chang Ta have erected an inscription as follows:

The majestic miraculous power of the goddess the Celestial Spouse, to whom by imperial command the title has been conferred of "Protector of the country and defender of the people whose miraculous power manifestly answers [prayers] and whose vast benevolence saves universally", is widely spread over the great sea and her virtuous achievements have been recorded in a most honourable manner in the Bureau of Sacrificial Worship. From the time when we, Cheng Ho and his companions, at the beginning of the Yung-lo period received the Imperial commission as envoys to the barbarians up till now seven voyages have taken place and each time we have commanded several tens of thousand government soldiers and more than a hundred ocean-going vessels. Starting from T'ai-ts'ang and taking the sea we have by way of the countries of Chan-ch'eng (Chapma), Hsien-lo (Siam), Kua-wa (Java), K'o-chih (Cochin) and Ku-li (Calicut) reached Hul-lu-mo-ssu (Ormuz) and other countries of the western regions, more than 3,000[196] countries in all, traversing more than one hundred thousand *li* of immense water spaces and beholding waves (gaping like the mouths of) whales, rising up to heaven, immense and (succeeding each other) endlessly. Now there was the drizzle of thick fogs, now steep windswept waves and in all those inconstant changes of the aspect of the ocean our sails, loftily unfurled like clouds, day and night continued their course, rapid like that of a star. Save by trusting in the divine power, how could we have found a tranquil crossing. When once it happened that we were in danger, as soon as we had pronounced the name of the goddess, the answer (to prayer) followed (swiftly) like an echo: suddenly there was a magic lantern in the mast and as soon as the miraculous light appeared the danger was becalmed.[197] Every one on the fleet, set at rest, felt assured that there was nothing to fear. This is in general terms what the merit of the goddess has accomplished.

On arriving in the outlying countries, those among the barbarian kings who were obstructing the "transforming influence" (of Chinese culture) and were disrespectful were captured alive, and brigands who gave themselves over to violence and plunder were exterminated. Consequently the sea route was purified and tranquillized and the natives, owing to this, were enabled quietly to pursue their avocations. All this is due to the aid of the goddess.

Formerly we have already reported the merits of the goddess in a memorial and have requested of the throne that a palace be erected at Nanking on the bank of the Dragon river where sacrificial worship is for ever to be continued. We have respectfully received an imperial commemorative composition in order to glorify the miraculous favours, thus bestowing the highest praise. However, wherever one goes there are places of residence for the miraculous power of the goddess. Thus the "temporary palace" at Liu-chia-chiang, built many years ago, has been repaired by us each time we have come hither. In the winter of the fifth year of Hsüan-tê (1430), having once more received a commission as envoys to the barbarian countries, we have moored our ships at the foot of the shrine and the soldiers of the government army have respectfully and sincerely assisted at the rites and the sacrifices have been continuous. We have added new improvements to the buildings of the goddess which vastly surpass the old established usage and we have rebuilt the shrine of the "Younger Sister of the Ch'ü Mountain" behind the palace, and have replaced the statue of the goddess in the principal hall with a new beautiful statue. Officers and common soldiers all gladly hastened hither to worship and there were some who could not control themselves (with joy). Could this have been brought about otherwise than by the sense of gratitude for the merit of the goddess, felt in men's hearts? Therefore we have written an inscription on stone and have moreover recorded the years and months of our voyages both going and returning in order to make these known for ever.[198]

I. In the third year of Yung-lo (1405) commanding the fleet we have gone to Ku-li (Calicut) and other countries. At that time the pirate Ch'en Tsu-yi and his followers were assembled at San-fo-ch'i (Palembang) where they plundered the native merchants. We captured that leader alive and returned in the fifth year (1407).

II. In the fifth year of Yung-lo (1407) commanding the fleet we went to Kua-wa (Java), Ku-li (Calicut), K'o-chih (Cochin) and Hsien-lo (Siam). The kings of these countries all presented as tribute local products, and precious birds and (rare) animals. We returned in the seventh year (1409).

III. In the seventh year of Yung-lo (1409), commanding the fleet we went to the countries (visited) before and took our route by the country of Hsi-lan-shan (Ceylon). Its king Ya-lieh-jo-nai-erh (Alagak-konāra) was guilty of a gross lack of respect and plotted against the fleet. Owing to the manifest answer (to prayer) of the divine power (the plot) was discovered and thereupon that king was captured alive. In the ninth year (1411) on our return he was presented (to the throne as a prisoner); subsequently he received the Imperial favour of returning to his own country.

IV. In the twelfth year of Yung-lo (1414), commanding the fleet, we went to Hu-lu-mo-ssu (Ormuz) and other countries. In the country of Su-men-ta-la (Samudra) the false king Su-kan-la (Sekan-dar) was marauding and invading his country. Its king had sent an envoy to the Palace Gates in order to lodge a complaint and to request assistance. Approaching with the official troops under our command we have exterminated and arrested (the rebels), and silently aided by the divine power we thereupon captured the false king alive. In the thirteenth year (1415), on our return he was presented (to the Emperor as a prisoner). In that year the king of the country of Man-la-chia (Malacca) came in person with his wife and sons to present tribute.

V. In the fifteenth year of Yung-lo (1417) commanding the fleet we visited the western regions.[199] The country of Hu-lu-mo-ssu (Ormuz) presented lions, leopards with gold spots and western horses. The country of A-tan (Aden) presented *ch'i-lin* of which the native name is *tsu-la-fa* (giraffe), as well as the long horned animal *ma-ha* (oryx). The country of Mu-ku-tu-shu (Mogadishu) presented *hua-fu-lu* ("striped" zebras) as well as lions. The country of Pu-la-wa (Brawa) presented camels which run one thousand *li* as well as camel-birds (ostriches). The countries of Kua-wa (Java) and Ku-li (Calicut) presented the animal *mi-li-kao*.[200] All presented local products the like of which had never been heard of before and sent the maternal uncle or the younger brother (of the king) to present a letter of homage written on gold leaf as well as tribute.

VI. In the nineteenth year of Yung-lo (1421) commanding the fleet we conducted the ambassadors from Hu-lu-mo-ssu (Ormuz) and the other countries, who had been in attendance at the capital for a long time, back to their countries. The kings of all these countries presented local products as tributes even more abundantly than previously.

VII. In the fifth year of Hsüan-tê (1430), starting once more for the barbarian countries) in order to make known the imperial commands, the fleet has anchored at the foot of the shrine and recalling how previously we have on several occasions received the benefits of the protection of the divine intelligence we have hereupon inscribed a text on stone.

Second Inscription[201]

Record of the miraculous answer (to prayer) of the goddess the Celestial Spouse.

The Imperial Ming Dynasty unifying seas and continents, surpassing the three dynasties even goes beyond the Han and T'ang dynasties. The countries beyond the horizon and from the ends of the earth have all become subjects and to the most western of the western or the most northern of the northern countries, however far they may be, the distance and the routes may be calculated. Thus the barbarians from beyond the seas, though their countries are truly distant, "with double translation" have come to audience bearing precious objects and presents.

The Emperor, approving of their loyalty and sincerity, has ordered us (Cheng) Ho and others at the head of several tens of thousands of officers and flag-troops to ascend more than one hundred large ships to go and confer presents on them in order to make manifest the transforming power of the (imperial) virtue and to treat distant people with kindness. From the third year of Yung-lo (1405) till now we have seven times received the commission of ambassadors to countries of the western ocean. The barbarian countries which we have visited are: by way of Chan-ch'eng (Champa), Chao-wa (Java), San-fo-ch'i (Palembang) and Hsien-lo (Siam) crossing straight over to Hsi-lan-shan (Ceylon) in South-India, Ku-li (Calicut), and K'o-chih (Cochin), we have gone to the western regions Hu-lu-mo-ssu (Hormuz), A-tan (Aden), Mu-ku-tu-shu (Mogadishu), altogether more than thirty countries large and small. We have traversed more than one hundred thousand *li* of immense water spaces and have beheld in the ocean huge waves like mountains rising sky-high, and we have set eyes on barbarian regions far away hidden in a blue transparency of light vapours, while our sails loftily unfurled like clouds day and night continued their course (rapid like that) of a star, traversing those savage waves as if we were treading a public thoroughfare. Truly this was due to the majesty and the good fortune of the Court and moreover we owe it to the protecting virtue of the divine Celestial Spouse.

The power of the goddess having indeed been manifested in previous times has been abundantly revealed in the present generation. In the midst of the rushing waters it happened that, when there was a hurricane, suddenly there was a divine lantern shining in the mast, and as soon as this miraculous light appeared the danger was appeased, so that even in the danger of capsizing one felt reassured that there was no cause for fear. When we arrived in the distant countries we captured alive those of the native kings who were not respectful and exterminated those barbarian robbers who were engaged in piracy, so that consequently the sea route was cleansed and pacified and the natives put their trust in it. All this is due to the favours of the goddess.

It is not easy to enumerate completely all the cases where the goddess has answered (prayers). Previously in a memorial to the Court we have requested that her virtue be registered in the Court of Sacrificial Worship and a temple be built at Nanking on the bank of the dragon river where regular sacrifices should be transmitted for ever. We have respectfully received an Imperial commemorative composition exalting the miraculous favours, which is the highest recompense and praise indeed. However, the miraculous power of the goddess resides wherever one goes. As for the temporary palace on the southern mountain at Ch'ang-lo, I have, at the head of the fleet, frequently resided there awaiting the (favourable) wind to set sail for the ocean. Thereupon in the tenth year of Yung-lo (1412) I reported in a memorial that the place where the government troops pray and report their success had already been completely put in order. On the right hand side (i.e. the west side) there was on the southern mountain a pagoda of very great antiquity which was in a neglected and dilapidated condition. On each visit repairs were made and after a lapse of several years the principal halls and meditation chambers now greatly surpass the former standard. This year in the spring having started once more for the barbarian countries I have moored the ships in this port and, having again repaired the halls of the Buddhas and the palaces of the gods with even more splendour, I furthermore resolved to spend funds for the building of a Precious Hall for the Three Pure ones to the left of the palace, to have wholly new and beautiful images of the gods sculpted and decorated, and to provide completely all the bells and drums and sacrificial utensils. It was declared unanimously that thus it would be possible to serve with the utmost reverence the heart of divine intelligence of Heaven and Earth, and all vowed that it should be thus, so that all gladly hasten hither to serve. The buildings, grand and beautiful, will be completed before long, the painted beams rise up to the clouds in a vigorous flight. Moreover there are green pine-trees and bamboo of kingfisher blue giving a pleasant shade on either side. The gods having a peaceful dwelling and men rejoicing, it surely is a remarkable spot. How would such a place and such people not all receive happiness and prosperity? If men are able to serve their prince with the exertion of all their loyalty then all things will be successfully established; if they are able to serve the gods with the utmost sincerity then all their prayers will be answered.

We, Cheng Ho and others, on the one hand have received the high favour of a gracious commission of our Sacred Lord, and on the other hand carry to the distant barbarians the benefits of respect and good faith (on their part). Commanding the multitudes on the fleet and (being responsible for) a quantity of money and valuables in the face of the violence of the winds and the nights our one fear is not to be able to succeed; how should we then dare not to serve our dynasty with exertion of all our loyalty and the gods with the utmost sincerity? How would it be possible not to realize what is the source of the tranquillity of the fleet and the troops[202] and the salvation on the voyage both going and returning? Therefore we have made manifest the virtue of the goddess on stone and have moreover recorded the years and months of the voyages to the barbarian countries and the return in order to leave (the memory) for ever.

I. In the third year of Yung-lo (1405) commanding the fleet we went to Ku-li (Calicut) and other countries. At that time the pirate Ch'en Tsu-yi had gathered his followers in the country of San-fo-ch'i (Palembang), where he plundered the native merchants. When he also advanced to resist our fleet, supernatural soldiers secretly came to the rescue so that after one beating of the drum he was annihilated. In the fifth year (1407) we returned.

II. In the fifth year of Yung-lo (1407) commanding the fleet we went to Chao-wa (Java), Ku-li (Calicut), K'o-chih (Cochin) and Hsien-lo (Siam). The kings of these countries all sent as tribute precious objects, precious birds and rare animals. In the seventh year (1409) we returned.

III. In the seventh year of Yung-lo (1409) commanding the fleet we went to the countries (visited) before and took our route by the country of Hsi-lan-shan (Ceylon). Its king Ya-lieh-k'u-nai-erh (Alagakkonara) was guilty of a gross lack of respect and plotted against the fleet. Owing to the manifest answer to prayer of the goddess (the plot) was discovered and thereupon that king was captured alive. In the ninth year (1411) on our return the king was presented (to the throne) (as a prisoner); subsequently he received the Imperial favour of returning to his own country.

IV. In the eleventh year[203] of Yung-lo (1413) commanding the fleet we went to Hu-lu-mo-ssu (Ormuz) and other countries. In the country of Su-men-ta-la (Samudra) there was a false king Su-kan-la (Sekandar) who was marauding and invading his country. Its king Tsai-nu-li-a-pi-ting (Zaynu-'l-Ābidin) had sent an envoy to the Palace Gates in order to lodge a complaint. We went thither with the official troups under our command and exterminated some and arrested (other rebels), and owing to the silent aid of the goddess we captured the false king alive. In the thirteenth year (1415) on our return he was presented (to the Emperor as a prisoner). In that year the king of the country of Man-la-chia (Malacca) came in person with his wife and son to present tribute.

V. In the fifteenth year of Yung-lo (1417) commanding the fleet we visited the western regions. The country of Hu-lu-mo-ssu (Ormuz) presented lions, leopards with gold spots and large western horses. The country of A-tan (Aden) presented ch'i-lin of which the native name is *Tsu-la-fa* (giraffe), as well as the long-horned animal *ma-ha* (oryx). The country of Mu-ku-tu-shu (Mogadishu) presented *hua-fu-lu* ("striped" zebras) as well as lions. The country of Pu-la-wa (Brawa) presented camels which run one thousand *li* as well as camel-birds (ostriches). The countries of Chao-wa (Java) and Ku-li (Calicut) presented the animal *mi-li-kao*. They all vied in presenting the marvellous objects preserved in the mountains or hidden in the seas and the beautiful treasures buried in the sand or deposited on the shores. Some sent a maternal uncle of the king, others a paternal uncle or a younger brother of the king in order to present a letter of homage written on gold leaf as well as tribute.

VI. In the nineteenth year of Yung-lo (1421) commanding the fleet we conducted the ambassadors from Hu-lu-mo-ssu (Ormuz) and the other countries who had been in attendance at the capital for a long time back to their countries. The kings of all these countries prepared even more tribute than previously.

VII. In the sixth year[204] of Hsüan-tê (1431) once more commanding the fleet we have left for the barbarian countries in order to read to them (an Imperial edict) and to confer presents.

We have anchored in this port awaiting a north wind to take the sea, and recalling how previously we have on several occasions received the benefits of the protection of the divine intelligence we have thus recorded an inscription in stone.

X

The Ending of the Chinese Expeditions to the Western Seas and Africa

After this, night descends for ever on these legendary ocean voyages, and on the life of Cheng Ho himself. Cordier—who in his *Histoire Générale de la Chine* merely says that "in the sixth moon of 1430 Cheng Ho was sent with Wang Ching-hung to Hormuz and other countries", without specifically mentioning the African coasts, adds that "returning in 1435, worn with age and fatigue" Cheng Ho "died soon afterwards".[205] Thus, as Pelliot also observes,[206] one can hardly accept the notion sometimes put forward that Cheng Ho died in 1431, during the seventh and last great expedition to the Western Ocean.

Hsüan-tê's imperial order (as is confirmed by Cheng Ho's biography) was issued in the fifth year of his reign, in the sixth moon (20th June–19th July 1430), but the actual date of sailing, as has been noted, must have been only at the beginning of 1432. For the return to Nanking the date of 22nd July 1433 is given, and there is no evidence for the idea that Cheng Ho died on the eve of departure or during the voyage. However, he could well have died just after the return, as Cordier states. It is noteworthy that a subsequent mission to Sumatra in 1434 was entrusted to the other Grand Eunuch Wang Ching-hung, who had been Cheng Ho's companion on the previous expeditions.

Why were the great sails "loftily unfurled like clouds" suddenly no longer hoisted to the wind of the vast ocean expanses? Why did the great naval shipyards, used to launching splendid ship after ship, with ever more masts and decks, gradually lapse into silence until in the end they ceased all activity towards the end of the fifteenth century? Why did imperial decree, which formerly had struck at the ships' cargoes and the commanders accused of exporting the treasured currency, now strike at the ships themselves, to stop their construction and limit their movements? What justification was there for this return to a drastic isolation on the part of a country which in nautical skills had surpassed all others, having mastery of the oceans and profitable commercial relations with the remotest peoples of other continents and other races?

One may bear in mind that when in the first decades of the sixteenth century the imperial edicts were issued which practically put an end to all real official maritime activity, the Portuguese already installed in Macao had not only sent out missionaries to spread the Gospel but had also established a jealous and ruthless monopoly of ocean trade.[207] One may also take the view, as some writers in fact have done, that a contributory cause of the cessation of contacts between China and the African world was the difficulty in communication resulting from the unintelligibility of Chinese speech and writing for the coastal population of Africa.[208]

Above all, however, one must bear in mind those motives of an ethical, religious, philosophical and cultural character which had the aim of keeping the values of a highly contemplative and speculative civilization free from contamination with the "barbarian" rest of the world.

The decision of Yung-lo's successor Hung-hsi to put an end to the ships seeking precious stones from across the Western Ocean was taken on the advice of Hsia Yün-chi, who from the outset had criticized such expeditions and had even been imprisoned for his obstinate opposition to them. On Yung-lo's death he ntaurally again insisted on the necessity of stopping such enterprises; and, after the brief interlude of Hung-hsi's reign, the latter's successor Hsüan-tê gave the following precise dispositions, as reported in the *Shih-lu:* "The ships for [seeking] precious stones, which go to the barbarian countries of the Western Ocean, shall all be stopped. If any of them is now anchored in Fu-chien or in T'ai-ts'ang, it shall return to Nanking without fail. The building of ships to go to the barbarian [countries] shall be everywhere stopped."[209]

The seventh expedition entrusted by the Emperor Hsüan-tê himself to Cheng Ho must in fact be considered a quite isolated episode, justified solely by consideration of the political prestige of the Celestial Empire in the most distant countries of the then known world. Duyvendak writes: "If China had continued Yung-lo's policy of encouraging foreign trade and overseas relations, the course of history might have been different."[210]

References to Cheng Ho's voyages, precisely because of the isolationist policy pursued by Yung-lo's successors, became more and more fragmentary and superficial, and were never to be found in the context of "China's glorious past".[211] The travel journals of Ma Huan, Fei Hsin and Kung Chen were never widely disseminated, and accounts in other books are scarce and difficult of access.

Cheng Ho and his companions must certainly have written down and submitted to the Emperor detailed reports on each voyage. But it seems that when in the Ch'eng-hua period (1465–87) the order was given to look for them in the imperial archives,[212] they could not be traced. In fact, the reports had previously been hidden away and burned by the Vice-President of the War Ministry, Liu Ta-hsia. When the President of the same Ministry, Hsiang Ching, expressed to Liu Ta-hsia his surprise at the disappearance of the documents, Liu observed: "The expeditions of the San Pao[213] to the Western Ocean wasted tens of myriads of money and grain, and moreover the people who met their deaths (on these expeditions) may be counted by the myriads. Although he returned with wonderful precious things, what benefit was it to the state? This was merely an action of bad government of which ministers should severely disapprove. Even if the old archives were still preserved they should be destroyed in order to suppress [a repetition of these things] at the root."[214]

But was this expansionist policy, and were these ocean ventures in particular, a real disaster for China from the human and the economic point of view?

Certainly, the *Li-tai T'ung-chien chi-lan* pronounces judgment against them: "The treasures which were squandered on these enterprises yielded no profit in return, while many of the soldiers of the expeditions perished in shipwrecks or were cast away on distant shores, so that the number that came back, after a matter of years, was not more than one or two out of every 10." However, one cannot fail to consider other evidence adduced by other scholars which shows this to be a mistaken view.

Thus Jung-pang Lo states that of more than 1,800 ocean-going ships built during the reign of Yung-lo, over 1,700 (including the "jewel ships", those of larger tonnage) were built in the first six years. The cost of building a large ocean vessel was equal to that of 1,000 *piculs* of rice, or about 350 taels of silver at that time.[215] Yet the revenue of Soochow district alone amounted to three million piculs, and that of the empire to 30 million.[216]

If then from the political and military and trade aspects this maritime vocation was on balance remunerative, enhancing China's prestige in distant lands and enriching the state coffers, what could be the real reasons behind the decline of Chinese maritime power and the ending of China's official contracts with the outside world?

During the Middle Ages there was a kind of pendular motion in China's policies and fortunes. After the death of Yung-lo, military reverses, the gradual and then hurried withdrawal from the most advanced naval bases, the increasing decline and abandonment of the fleet that had been the pride of the first two Ming emperors, and the return to a form of slavish and inert Confucian conformism clipped the wings of any bold initiative or vital impulse.

The prime causes of this retreat from the sea are to be sought in two sets of factors, physical and psychological. On the one hand the Chinese nation, or at least those who were responsible for it, was again turning north-westwards, which resulted in a heightening of continental interests and a wakening of maritime ones. On the other hand "the blind adherence to works of the Chu Hsi School of Sung Confucianism without acquiring their master's curiosity about nature and the world outside" reinforced China's addiction to an empty cultural superiority which taught men to repress their worldly instincts and to be happy with the destiny to which Heaven had called them.[217]

A memorandum submitted to the Emperor in 1426 by one of his ministers shows clearly how this attitude now pervaded the highest circles, expressing a policy which was more and more to influence imperial decisions: "Your minister hopes that Your Majesty . . . would not indulge in military pursuits nor glorify the sending of expeditions to distant countries. Abandon the barren lands abroad and give the people of China a respite so that they could devote themselves to husbandry and to the schools. Thus, there would be no wars and suffering on the frontier and no murmuring in the villages, the commanders would not seek fame and the soldiers would not sacrifice their lives abroad, the people from afar would voluntarily submit and distant lands would come into our fold, and our dynasty would last for ten thousand generations."[218]

Confident of spiritual and material self-sufficiency, Yung-lo's successors laid stress on agriculture to the detriment of trade and industry. They overdid the importance of classical studies, winning men away from the pursuit of science; and they exalted literature, casting contempt on all who pursued the arts of warfare. "Officials of this turn of mind deliberately destroyed the charts used in Cheng Ho's voyages to forestall further naval expeditions. They so discouraged shipbuilding that in a book published in 1553, barely a hundred and twenty years after Cheng's last voyage, came the admission that the art of building 'treasure ships' was lost. Those for whom the call of the sea remained strong were faced with government bans on emigration and on participation by private individuals in foreign trade."[219]

The idea that the state should no longer engage in commercial enterprises, far less exhaust itself in wars beyond its borders, but should win respect and glory by intellectual conquests and spiritual concentration was, finally, more than a conviction of the moment; it was the outcome of a political and economic decay now destined to undermine the nation.

The squandering of public money, one of the charges brought

against the voyages of the "jewel ships", did not in fact cease with the ending of these expeditions. Vast assignments of funds were voted for totally unproductive ends, such as disproportionate appanages for the imperial princes, and the construction of a grandiose mausoleum for defunct Emperors.[220]

However, the ending of the naval expeditions which, under Cheng Ho, had attained the shores of Africa and conferred on the Chinese Court unprecedented lustre and renown did not mark the ending of all contacts with the remote lands of the West. The Ming History (*Ming-shih*) refers to another mission carried out after Cheng Ho's last voyage of 1431–33, although in the opposite direction, namely from Egypt to China.

"Sixth year, ninth moon, Kêng-shên (12th October 1441). The ruler of Mi-hsi-erh (Misr) and other territories, Su-lu-t'an A-shih-la-fy and others, dispatched as envoys Sai-i-ta-li (Sayyid Ali) and others, also the *chih-hui* (commander) of the chieftainship of Fu-yü, A-li-t'ai and others—all came to the court with tribute of mules, horses, and various products of their localities. A banquet was proffered to them together with gifts of silk stuffs and garments, each according to their different status." They left again in the same year, in the second month, on 10th November 1441.[221]

These or other occasional episodes, the result of initiatives not by China but by rulers of distant foreign countries, cannot however be considered as an active continuation of official relations with the outside world on the part of the Chinese imperial Court.

The salient point is the dynamism of private enterprise which, once the commerial monopoly exercised by the state had ended, saw new horizons opening and succeeded in some measure in keeping alive the traffic that had flourished so well under the Sung and Yüan Emperors and in the early Ming period. Indeed, those of the merchants and Court dignitaries themselves who were used to acquiring conspicuous profits from maritime trade by no means resigned themselves to giving up these activities. More than a few not too scrupulous officials and eunuchs employed in the supervision of the merchants' shipping began to invest their capital in this kind of business. They had built on their own account large vessels which attracted the men of the coastal districts, nurtured in a long maritime tradition, both as seamen and as merchants.

In short, seagoing trade in private hands replaced that of the state, securing vast profits to its investors, who became the most jealous opponents and saboteurs of any possible restoration of the government trade monopoly. As Jung-pang Lo observes, they were able to promote their own interests thanks to their powerful connections in Peking, and fostered lively opposition on the part of influential officials to any attempt to resume official maritime expeditions.[222]

But the fact remained that what had become extinguished for ever was the power of the imperial navy which had enabled China, at a certain point in her history, to dominate unchallenged the sea routes of southern Asia and "the western seas".

The policy of withdrawal initiated by Yung-lo's successors was to produce, within a few years, calamitous consequences. On the accession of the Emperor Cheng-t'ung in 1436 an edict was promulgated which not only prohibited the construction of ships for overseas voyages, but even put an end to the building of warships and armaments.

The picture drawn by Jung-pang Lo is sadly realistic: "The situation was further aggravated by the diversion of naval craft to nonmilitary uses such as grain conveyance. . . . In 1509, the authorities decreed that ships damaged by storms were not to be repaired, and in 1524 an imperial edict halted the construction of sea-going ships at Teng-chou in order to relieve the burden of the people. . . . The large-size, deep-draughted transports were gradually replaced by smaller, flat-bottom barges. The small number of transports built in government dockyards for maritime service were far inferior in construction to the privately-built merchant ships. . . . The largest warships of the Ming navy in the beginning of the sixteenth century were 400-*liao* (units) vessels with a crew of a hundred. . . . Parallelling the physical decay of the navy was the demoralization of the personnel. . . . In the early Ming period, the men of the navy who sailed out to sea received an additional subsidy which amounted to a third of their pay and those who went abroad in the naval expeditions were liberally rewarded. . . . [Now] from fighting men they were reduced to the status of stevedores. . . . Desertion was heavy. Of the garrison of 4,068 men at the Feng-huo base, 3,000 deserted; of the 4,700 men at Hsiao-ch'eng, 2,557 deserted; of the 3,424 men at Wu-hsü, 1,468 deserted; and of the 1,812 men at T'ung-shan, 1,192 deserted. . . .

"Against a background of general deterioration and widespread distress, this was the mentality which prompted Yang Shih-ch'i to urge a retreat from Annam on the ground that it was a virtuous act, Chou Kan to advocate the withdrawal of the island naval bases to reduce the cost of maintenance, and Liu Ta-hsia to destroy the sea-charts to frustrate the dispatch of what he claimed to be costly expeditions.

"It took China three centuries to ascend to the position of maritime greatness but the descent was swift and easy To be sure, the coastal residents continued to engage in seafaring and trade and the government still maintained naval forces which saw much action during the sixteenth and seventeenth centuries, but Chinese sea power never regained the prominent position it occupied during the late Sung, Yüan and, particularly, the early Ming periods."[223]

In contrast to the conduct of Egyptians, Phoenicians, Arabs and Persians, before Cheng Ho's expeditions, and to the subsequent policies of Portuguese, British, French, Germans and Italians, the Chinese confined themselves to appearing on the coast of East Africa, without any aim of exerting direct influence on the life and destinies of the local populations. They were neither conquerors nor emigrants in search of new homes, but only able navigators and merchants who made known to remote countries the illustrious name and gracious commands of the Son of Heaven.

Even under Yung-lo, China's direct traffic with Africa was not so active or consistent as that between Africa and the nearer and more interested peoples of the Arabian peninsula and the Persian Gulf. So far as is known at the present, no cohesive Chinese community at that time took up permanent residence in the inhabited centres of Africa's eastern coasts. Schwarz's strange theories about cultural and racial influences deriving from the spectacular Chinese expeditions and the prolonged sojourns of tens of thousand of Chinese in the district of Inyanga and on the Usambara plateau between the tenth and twelfth centuries rest at present on no convincing evidence.

Grottanelli has put the matter as follows: "These were isolated seafaring enterprises which left practically no trace in the culture of the coastal peoples, let alone their ethnic composition. The Chinese who in later times disembarked on the coast of East Africa, and occasionally settled there, were isolated arrivals, or came in small groups on Middle Eastern vessels. We find Chinese today in Cape Province and in Androy, in scattered groups in the southernmost mainland or island localities of Africa. Two Chinese recently joined the Bajun islands community; others may have preceeded them here or at other points on the east coast, becoming fused with other races in the course of generations."[224]

Meanwhile, apart from some coins, some porcelain and some fragments of Chinese pottery, the sporadic maritime contacts of former times, and in particular those organized with such *éclat* by Cheng Ho, have left few visible traces.

Yet we have before us a page of the history of human relations which can still yield new and surprising revelations. The writer of these modest notes will feel they have achieved one of their main purposes if they have the effect of stimulating further study and research in this field.

References

1. J. J. L. Duyvendak, *China's Discovery of Africa*. Lectures given at the University of London on 22nd and 23rd January 1947, London, Probsthain, 1949, p. 5. Duyvendak died in 1954. Since his death Chinese scholars have made valuable direct or indirect contributions to the subject; they include Jung-pang Lo, Wu Chi-hua, Wang Gung-wu, Pao Tsun-p'eng, Chuang Wei-chi, Chou Shin-te, Chuang Wei and others. For the important studies by V. Vel'gus, see bibliography.

2. Pirone, p. 38; Duyvendak, op. cit., p. 20.

3. Duyvendak, op. cit., p. 26: "All these notices on countries in Africa are based on hearsay, and there is no indication that the Chinese themselves ever reached the African shores. We now come to a period in which they actually entered into direct relations with several African countries, in which they indeed really discovered Africa for themselves." Cfr. P. Pelliot in *T'oung Pao*, vol. XIII, No. 3, July 1912, p. 461.

4. Schwarz, pp. 176-8.

5. One cannot exclude the possibility of further researches in the Inyanga and Usambra areas, discussed by Schwarz, leading to new and interesting discoveries.

6. Cfr. *inter alia:* Duyvendak, *China's Discovery*, and "The true dates"; and Pelliot, "Les grands voyages".

7. Cheng Ho's first expeditions demonstrated this, serving as they did to reduce to obedience or subjection kings or robbers who had rebelled against the supreme imperial authority.

8. See Deschamps; Hollingsworth, p. 56; and Reusch.

9. See Hudson and Teggart: Hirth's *China and the Roman Orient* and *Story of Chang K'ién* (Chang K'ién, during the *chien-yüan* period—140–134 BC—reached the region of Bactria, in present Afghanistan and even reached Syria); Richthofen, Schoff, Herrmann's *Die Verkehrswege*, Needham (vol. 1) and Duyvendak (*China's Discovery*, pp. 5–9 and 24–6).

10. Pelliot (review of *Chau Ju-kua*, p. 461) writes: "Although it seems certain that in ancient times the Chinese at a certain stage in their voyage transferred on to ships of the 'barbarians', it seems no less certain that at the beginning of the Christian Era, by order of the Court, a Chinese mission traversed the whole of the Indian Ocean."

    See also Mills, p. 5; Pelliot *T'oung Pao*, vol. XVI, 1915, pp. 690–1 and "Less anciens rapports", pp. 21–2; Hirth, "Early Chinese notices"; Chavannes, "Les pays d'occident".

11. Duyvendak, *China's Discovery*, p. 9.

12. Pelliot, *T'oung Pao*, vol. XIII, 1912, pp. 457–461.

13. Duyvendak, *China's Discovery*, pp. 10–11; Herrmann, *Ein Seeverkehr*, p. 553; and Wheatley.

14. Davidson, p. 157. Davidson makes detailed mention of Fa Hsien's *Travels* (see bibliography).

15. Mills, p. 6, citing Worcester.

16. Kuwabara. According to Kuwabara (pp. 1–2) P'u Shou-kêng was superintendent of the office for merchant shipping, known as T'i-chü-shih-po-ssu. He was of Arab origin and enjoyed much influence as a result of his post.

17. Davidson, p. 159. Chu Yu's *P'ing-chou k'o-t'an* of 1119, partly based on information obtained from Chu Yu's father who had been Governor of Canton from 1099 to 1102, states that pearls, camphor and all articles of fine quality were charged 10 per cent, and tortoiseshell, sandal-wood and all

F

coarse grade articles 30 per cent. After these charges were paid the remainder belonged to the merchants themselves. Ivory tusks of 30 catties or over (about 35–45 pounds) as well as gum olibanum, had to be disposed of in the official market. As a result, merchants having large ivory tusks cut them in pieces of three catties or less, so that they could sell them as they wished, since the official market prices were extremely unfavourable to the merchants. Any attempt to evade the clearance dues was punished by confiscation of the entire cargo (Duyvendak, *China's Discovery*, pp. 16–17). On the maritime customs system, see Hirth and Rockhill's *Chau Ju-kua*: pp. 20–1 give various data about the duties, taken from the *P'ing-chou k'o-t'an*. Under the Yüan dynasty the duties were lower, as can be gathered from Marco Polo. However, what with transport costs and the duties payable to the Great Khan, the merchant had to surrencer a good half of his investment. Nevertheless, he could recoup with the profits of the remaining half and be well enough rewarded to return with another cargo. See also Kuwabara, p. 3 and notes, and Davidson, p. 159.

18. See also Davidson, p. 157.
19. Kuwabara, note 23, pp. 26–7.
20. Mills, p. 8.
21. Kuwabara, note 22, p. 24.
22. Kuwabara, p. 3.
23. Ch'üan-chou corresponds to the Zaytun of the Arabs. It appears under this name in Abul Fida, and also in Marco Polo. The great port excited the admiration of Arab and Venetian alike, and also of Franciscan missionaries. All foreign communities—Indian, Persian or Arab—were permitted to follow their own customs and religion and to settle in their own quarter, known as *Fan-fang*, foreign quarter. L. Carrington Goodrich writes ("Recent discoveries", p. 171): "Every student of Asiatic history has heard of Zayton, or Ch'üan-chou, the famous port on the south-east coast of China, especially active during the years *ca* 900 to 1474. At the height of its prosperity the city and its suburbs must have had a population close to half a million souls. . . . Ships connected it with all parts of the Asiatic and Mediterranean and doubtless East African worlds." Frate Odorico da Pordenone wrote that the city was twice as large as Bologna in population. Excavations conducted by Professor J. Foster and Chuang Wei have confirmed the vast extent of this maritime metropolis, and have brought to light the old foreign quarters with their mosques, cemeteries and Muslim tombs. At Zaytun there is also an inscription by Cheng Ho which records that the Grand Eunuch burned votive incense here on 31st March 1417 (D. H. Smith). See also Kuwabara, p. 33 and Needham, vol. I. p. 180.
24. Duyvendak, *China's Discovery*, p. 16, comments: "We do not, unfortunately, know how much a unit was, different for the different types of articles, but the figures gives us a fair idea of the enormous increase. In order to find a market for these goods the officials were ordered to encourage the people to buy them with 'gold', 'piece goods, rice, and straw'." See also Hirth and Rockhill, pp. 21–2 and note 4, p. 19.
25. The word *zenj* in Persian means "black". It appears for the first time in the works of Ptolemy (100–178), and the Arab geographers began to use it at the end of the ninth century. Persian writers often refer to the coast of East Africa as "the land of the *zenj*", or "land of the blacks". The whole coast was called Zenjibar (the Arabic *barr* signifying "land"); hence Zanzibar, *pars pro toto*. See Hollingsworth, p. 33; Reusch, p. 115; and Stigand, Pearce and Ingham. The most significant document is undoubtedly the "book of Zinj" translated by Cerulli from two MSS, one owned in

1925 by the Qadi of Kisimayu, and the copy of a text obtained at Vitu by Alice Werner (Cerulli, pp. 231–357). See also Oliver and Fage, p. 98: "All the way down the coastline of Somaliland, Kenya, and Tanganyika, there sprouted urbanized Islamic communities, building in stone or coral rag, and wealthy enough, for example, to import such luxury goods as the stoneware of Siam and the porcelain of Late Sung and early Ming China."

26. Jung-pang Lo ("*The decline*", pp. 154–5) observes that in the Ming period the bulk of payments in money were effected in paper currency, which, given China's prestige under the first two emperors, Hung-wu and Yung-lo, was willingly accepted even in foreign countries and enjoyed a good rate of exchange.

27. See Duyvendak, *China's Discovery*, p. 32: "There was, in the capital, an Imperial Zoological Garden in which such rarities were kept, and when expeditions returned they were reguarly followed by a string of foreign ambassadors (including, on one occasion, even an ambassador from 'Misr', Egypt) with their gifts of lions, tigers, oryxes, nilgaus, zebras, ostriches, etc." See also Pirone, p. 39, and Girace.

28. Kuwabara, note 23, pp. 26–7; Duyvendak, p. 17; Davidson, p. 170.

29. Duyvendak, *China's Discovery*, p. 17, and Kuwabara, note 22, pp. 24–5.

30. Kuwabara observes that, in practice, all the prohibitions and the accompanying scale of severe punishments remained a dead letter.

31. See pp. 43–51 of the present study.

32. Jung-pang Lo, "The decline", p. 154.

33. Kuwabara, pp. 35–6, and Jung-pang Lo, "The emergence", p. 499.

34. See, among others, Fairgrieve, p. 242, and Eldridge, p. 47. In contrast to the conventional view of China as a country traditionally averse to grand maritime ventures, one finds the fantastic but recurrent theory, resuscitated by Professor Chu Shien-tai of the University of Peking, as reported in the Hong Kong *Wen Wei Po* of June 1962, that America was not discovered by Christopher Columbus in 1492 but by five Chinese in 459. According to ancient Chinese writings, the first traveller from overseas to set foot on the American continent was a young Buddhist monk named Wai Sum, who had sailed from China with four companions past the Kurile and Aleutian islands and as far as Mexico. He returned to China forty years later and died in about 518.

Appendix to Reference 34

I am grateful to Professor Hulsewé for some further details about the claim that the American continent was discovered by Wai Sum and his companions about a thousand years before the voyage of Christopher Columbus. (Wai Sum is the Cantonese version of the Peking Chinese name of the Buddhist mink Hui-shen.) The story is a hardy perennial. It was a Western scholar who first produced it, the eighteenth-century Sinologist de Guignes, in "Recherches sur les navigations des Chinois du côté de l'Amérique", *Mémoires de l'Académie des Inscriptions*, fasc. XXVIII, 1761, pp. 505–25. Gustav Schlegel ("Problèmes géographiques", *T'oung Pao*, vol. III, 1892, pp. 101 ff.) listed articles and books on the subject. The matter was later taken up by B. Laufer in *T'oung Pao*, vol. XVI, 1915, pp. 198 ff. For an authoritative account of the matter, see L. C. Goodrich, "China's first knowledge of the Americas", *Geographical Review* (New York), vol. XXVIII, pp. 400 ff.

35. Jung-pang Lo, "The emergence", p. 489.

36. Ibid., p. 490. Jung-pang Lo also notes that a strong naval policy had been

called for by many Sung officials since 1129, offensive as well as defensive programmes being envisaged.

37. Ibid., p. 491.

38. Needham, vol. IV, part 1, p. 333. For Chinese nautical aids, see *idem*, vol. 1, pp. 128, 135 and 209; vol. II, p. 310 f.; vol. IV, pp. 249–313 and 330–4.

Duyvendak writes: "In European literature the first authentic record of it appears at the end of the twelfth or the beginning of the thirteenth century, and in Arabic literature no earlier mention has been found. Leaving aside earlier references, the polarity of the magnetic needle, as well as its declination, were certainly known in the eighth century, when the Buddhist priest and astronomer Yi-hsing mentioned both properties." Jung-pang Lo ("The emergence", p. 500) observes: "Maritime commerce and naval wars spurred the development of technology and the expansion of geographical knowledge. They encouraged the opening of ports and dredging of harbours, they advanced the art of navigation by such means as the mariner's compass and star and sea charts, and they furthered the publication of treatises on tides and currents and maps of foreign countries." See also Kuwabara, note 31, pp. 68–70.

39. Schwarz, however (p. 177), denies this manoeuvrability of the Chinese junks: "The clumsy nature of the yards and mat sails prevented the ships from tacking against the wind. The big capital ones had a complement of rowers who could be called upon to manoeuvre in times of difficulty, but the ships were too large for this procedure to be adopted for any length of time."

40. On this point also Needham's work (and in particular the unpublished third section of Vol. IV) may clarify many still obscure points. Davidson gives a rather odd and confused account of the matter when he writes (p. 157): "Their taut mat-sails are described as going round the masts like a door on its hinges, thus enabling ships to beat up to windward in a manner beyond the reach of Mediterranean sailors for a long time thereafter. These ocean-going vessels with their pivoting sails were known as 'boring into the wind' ships'." In reality the sail used on the Chinese vessels seems to have been similar in essentials to the Italian "vela adriatica". This is spread between two yards, the sloping gaff on top and the boom below. It is hoisted by pulleys to the masthead, to which it is secured. The sheet or "tack" which secures the boom to the deck, forward, allows it to pivot round the boom; it could describe a complete circle but for the sheet (Italian *scotta*) held by the steersman, which controls the ship as the bridle controls a horse.

The only sails which one can compare, as Davidson does, to a door turning on its hinges are either lug-sails, which however are secured to the mast at the side, or else the Bermuda rig, in which of course there is no gaff at the top and the end of the boom turns on the mast. One may add that sails spread between two yards, or those of the Bermuda type, permit better control of their angle to the wind, enabling the vessel to beat up against the wind. The more ancient types of sail, like the lateen, with only a top yard, gave poorer control; the sails ballooned and much of the sail spread was ineffective. Such vessels relied on a following wind, and had to spend long periods in harbour waiting for favourable winds. The two-yard sails and the Bermuda type were thus designed precisely for sailing *into* the wind. It seems very unlikely that the Chinese were the first to adopt this system. Nautical advances can almost always be traced back to the peoples of Oceania, who as modern ethnology has ascertained were the finest seamen in history. Their fast double or triple-hulled craft could sometimes do over 25 knots under sail. It is very probable that it was from them that the Chinese learnt the principles of seamanship, to which they added their own experience in the art of building in timber.

On the sailing rigs used by the Chinese, especially from the Sung period onward, see Kuwabara, note 31, p. 67, and Hirth and Rockhill, p. 30. The information is mainly taken from Chu Yu's *P'ing chou k'o-t'an*.

41. Audemard, p. 25, writes: "At that period most European ships did not have rudders; transverse oars were used to steer the vessel." For other details on the structure and handling of Chinese ships see Kuwabara, note 31, pp. 66–8.

42. Marco Polo, *Il Milione*, first complete edition, ed. Luigi Foscolo Benedetto, Florence, Leo S. Olschki, 1928, pp. 161–2.

43. For Yule's English translation of *Il Milione*, see bibliography under Yule.

44. There was generally a larger or principal anchor (*cheng-ting*) and a smaller or auxiliary anchor (*fu-ting*).

45. See *Voyage d'Ibn Batoutah*, texte arabe accompagné d'une traduction par C. Defremery et le Dr. B. F. Sanguinetti, Société Asiatique de Paris, 1958, vol. IV. The word "Abyssinians" here presumably means Africans in general, and more precisely the slaves whom the Arabs and Persians sold in the Chinese market. Jung-pang Lo, "The emergence", p. 500, states: "The ships of the Chinese, by contrast [with those of the Arabs] were ocean liners boasting staterooms, wineshops, and the service of negro stewards." Arab vessels at this time "were still flimsy craft lashed together with ropes".

46. Davidson, p. 163. The "Sung History" distinguished three types of vessels, according to a classification adopted from the T'ang dynasty onwards. The ships of larger burden, called by Duyvendak "One-mast ships", were of 1,000 *po-lam* burden; those of the second type were a third larger; and those of the third type were a third larger still. Ibn Battuta says that the Chinese ships are of three types, the large *gunuk* (singular *gunk; ch'uan*, "junk", in Chinese); the medium *zau* (*hsiao* in Chinese); and the small *ka-kam* (*hua-hang* in Chinese). Audemard (p. 27) reports some details given by Frate Giordano of the structure of the big junks and of Marco Polo's voyage. When the latter reached Singuy (Kiu-kiang) on the Yangtse he saw not less than 15,000 craft, of about 4,000 cantars (a cantar being about a hundredweight) or even of 12,000 cantars (i.e. 200 to 600 tons). See also Jung-pang Lo, "The emergence", pp. 489–503, and "The decline", pp. 149–68.

47. Davidson, p. 162.

48. Audemard, p. 25.

49. Ibid.

50. Audemard, p. 19.

51. Duyvendak, "Voyages de Tcheng Houo". The passages relating to Africa translated by Duyvendak comprise: (*a*) *Ming-shih*, 304, 2v–3r, chronological section, and ditto, 326, documentary section containing brief description of the Somali coastal centres: Mogadishu, 7v; Giumbo, 8r; (Aden, 8r–9r); La-sa, 9r; (*b*) a brief passage of the *Ta Ming-hui-tien* (chap. 98, 11v, of the edition of 1511) about the country of Malindi; (*c*) the two versions above cited of Fei Hsin's travel journal *Hsing-ch'a sheng-lan*; (*d*) a brief extract of the *Wu-hsueh-pien* (chap. 68, 41v) of Cheng Ch'iao concerning Malindi; (*e*) some passages of the inscription of Ch'ang-lo; (*g*) the sea map based on the voyages of Cheng Ho.

52. Kuwabara, pp. 35–6.

53. Speaking of Ibn Battuta's visit to India, Schwarz (p. 178) refers to the junks seen by him at Calicut "with their mat sails standing in the wind

while they lay at anchor. Thence they went to the south coast of Arabia, and then down the African coast, calling at all ports as far as Sofala; beyond was 'el mar scuro', whence no one returned."

54. Schwarz, pp. 177 and 178–9.

55. Schwarz, pp. 179–80.

56. Fripp, "A note", pp. 88–96.

57. Fripp, "Chinese Medieval trade", p. 18.

58. Schwarz, p. 181.

59. Jung-pang Lo, "The emergence", pp. 489 ff.

60. Duyvendak, *China's Discovery*, pp. 8 and 12; see also Hirth, "Early Chinese notices", and Chavannes, ed., "Les pays d'Occident".

61. Strandes, p. 88, note 1.

62. Ingrams, p. 93.

63. The text of the *Yu-yang tsa-tsu* has been translated by Hirth (see Hirth, "Early Chinese notices"). Oliver and Fage write (p. 97): "A ninth-century Chinese work clearly describes the contrast between the pastoral Somali, who grew no grain and drank the milk and blood of their cattle, and the wild blacks of Mo Lin, which is probably to be identified with Malindi on the Kenya coast."

64. Duyvendak, *China's Discovery*, pp, 13–14. Hirth ("Early Chinese notices", p. 48) says that there should be no doubts about the identification of *Po-pa-li* with Berbera, (a) because of the phonetic resemblance, (b) because ivory and ambergris were considered the principal products of that country, and (c) because Chao Ju-Kua's *Chu-fan-chih* (probably mid-twelfth century unmistakably refers to the same country, although he calls it *Pi-pa-lo*.

65. The *Hsin T'ang-shu*, or "New T'ang History", is one of the vast dynastic histories which also contains geographical chapters on China and descriptive accounts of foreign countries. It states (chap. 221, p. 19): "South-west [of the Arabs] is the sea and in the sea are the tribes of Po-pa-li. These tribes are not subject to any country. They do not cultivate grain, but live on meat and drink a mixture of milk and cow's blood; they do not wear clothes but cover their bodies with sheepskins. Their women are intelligent and handsone. The country produces a great quantity of ivory and incense, o-mo [in Cantonese o-mut = omur, for the Persian ambar, 'ambergris']. When merchants travelling from Po-ssi [Persia] want to go there to trade, they have to go in groups of several thousand persons, and after offering pieces of material and swearing a solemn oath (the oath of blood) they proceed to do their business." See also Hirth, "Early Chinese notices", p. 47.

66. See also Duyvendak, *China's Discovery*, p. 15 and footnote 2: "The identification is certain, for the name occurs in the Ming History where there can be no doubt as to its identity." For references to Ma-lin in the *Ming-shih*, see footnote 51 above.

67. Hirth and Rockhill, pp. 35–7.

68. Hirth and Rockhill, p. 122.

69. Hirth and Rockhill, part 1, 36, pp. 144–5.

70. Hirth and Rockhill, pp. 114–54. Among the "The countries situated in the sea" are also mentioned Sicily (Ssù-chia-li-yeh, part 1, 38, 7, pp. 153–4) and the southern coast of Spain (M-lan-p'i or Murabit, part 1, 35, pp. 142–3).

71. Reusch, pp. 156–7.

72. Ingrams, pp. 92–3.

73. For accounts of the monumental ruins of Zanzibar and Pemba, and in particular of Ras Mkumbuu on Pemba island, see Pearce, pp. 363–74; Ingrams, pp. 136–44; Kirkman, "Excavations at Ras Mkumbuu", pp. 161–78.

74. Ingrams, pp. 93–4.
75. Coupland, pp. 33–4. (There is an error in either the name of the Emperor or the date; in 976 the Sung dynasty was ruling.)
76. Duyvendak, *China's Discovery*, p. 23.
77. Hirth and Rockhill, pp. 31 and 48. A *tael* or *liang* equalled 579·84 grammes of silver. A *tael* was 1,000 *ch'ien*, metal coins with a square hole in the centre which were strung together to form a "string". When under the Ming dynasty metal coinage was almost entirely replaced by paper, "strings" were represented on the banknotes.
78. Duyvendak, *China's Discovery*, p. 24.
79. Hirth and Rockhill, part 1, 25, pp. 128–9. The four departmental cities or *chou* are to be identified, according to Hirth and Rockhill, with Berbera, Zeila, Mogadishu and perhaps Brava. The translation of the passage concerning Pi-p'a-lo is also given by Duyvendak (pp. 14–15).
80. The *li* is a Chinese measure corresponding to 1,890 feet, but it varied slightly in different periods.
81. Duyvendak, *China's Discovery*, pp. 20–2.
82. See also Grottanelli, pp. 65–6.
83. See among others Duyvendak, "Sailing directions", pp. 230–7; Needham, vol. III, pp. 225–90.
84. Duyvendak, *China's Discovery*, p. 31, footnote 3. Two interesting examples of the earliest Chinese cartography were published in 1903 by Chavennes (see bibliography). The two maps, the originals of which were carved in stone, are in the museum in Hsi-an. Map A is entitled "Map of China and of the Foreign Countries", but in fact it only shows China and part of Korea, the "foreign countries" only being listed in notes attached to the four cardinal points of the map itself (they include the country of the Ta-Shih, or Arabs). These notes include the statement: "In the time of Emperor Wu (140–187 BC) of the Han dynasty Chang Ch'ien opened the road to the countries of the West, entering into relations with 36 realms." Map B is entitled "Map of the Footsteps of Yu". Both maps date to 1137.

The representation of Africa in triangular shape at such an early period— whether from knowledge or from intuition —is surely remarkable, particularly if one thinks of the first maps or charts produced in Europe: notably the first map of Africa of Martin Sanudo (1321); the Atlante Nautico (1351), better known as "Gaddiano 9", in which Africa is very conspicuous with an outline tending to the trapezoidal; the Planisfero of Andrea Bianco of 1436, and that of Giovanni Leardo of 1452, notable for its better information about southern Africa; the famous Mappamondo secretly done at Venice by Fra Mauro Camaldolese for Prince Henry the Navigator in 1459, especially interesting for its geographical details of West Africa and Ethiopian regions; and finally Giacomo Gastaldi's Map of Africa of 1564 which, in its realistic outline of the continent, foreshadowed modern cartography. While admiring the precocious example of Chinese cartography to which Fuchs draws attention, one should not forget that the Greco-Egyptian author of the *Periplus of the Erythrean Sea* in 60 BC (or according to other authorities, such as Reinaud and Pirenne, around AD 225) makes a felicitous allusion to the real shape of Africa at the end of his account of the markets of the coast of Azania or East Africa: "And these markets of Azania . . . are in fact the last of the Continent, for beyond these places the unexplored ocean turns westward and joins the western sea" (the Atlantic Ocean).
85. For the historical background of the Mongol conquest and the establishment of the Ming dynasty by Chu Yuan-chang, see works by Cordier; Fairbank and Reischauer; and Franke, vol. IV, pp. 595 ff. and vol. V,

pp. 358 ff. For the events which led to the downfall of the Sung dynasty and the tragic end of Prince Ti-ping, see vol. IV, pp. 314–49.

86. According to the *Yüan-shih*, or *History of the Yüan Dynasty*, the Mongol Court in 1279 ordered the construction of 1,500 ships; this was increased in 1281 to 3,000 ships and in 1293 to 4,000. The invasion of Japan in 1281 was undertaken with 4,400 ships; those of Champa and of Tongking, between 1283 and 1288, with 800 ships; and the expedition against Java in 1293 with 1,000 ships. See Jung-pang Lo, "The emergence", p. 493. Mills (p. 10), quoting Chang T'ien-tsê's *Sino-Portuguese Trade* (1934), says that in 1284 the Chinese government tried to increase the profits deriving from foreign trade, and to this end built ships, recruited men, provided them with capital and invited them to trade in foreign countries. Private trade was banned on pain of severe punishments; but in fact the repeated prohibitions had no effect.

87. Chu Yüan-chang's achievement as a liberator and the founder of a dynasty which initially gave China an unprecedented military strength and capacity for expansion, and subsequently promoted its culture and art, recalls the similar achievement of the marabout Abdullah Ibn Yasin who with his monks set forth from his monastery on the river Senegal in 1042 to conquer in the name of Islam the whole of the western Sahara, later turning to northern Africa and crossing to the Iberian peninsula to give rise to the great empire of the Almoravids.

88. Duyvendak, *China's Discovery*, p. 26.

89. Ibid., pp. 26–7.

90. Needham, vol. I, pp. 143–4.

91. Cordier, vol. III, pp. 30–3. In fact, this is not a name but a title meaning "The Eunuch of the Three Jewels".

92. See also Needham, vol. I, pp. 556–7.

93. Liu-chai Chiang was very close to the site of the present Shanghai.

94. Pelliot, "Notes additionelles", pp. 304–5.

95. The Zinj empire, founded by Ali Ibn Hasan in 975–6, was at this period ruled by the pious Husayn Ibn Sulayman, who had succeeded Sulayman Ibn Sulayman in 1392–3.

96. Duyvendak, "The true dates", pp. 399–412, and idem, *China's Discovery*, pp. 32–3.

97. Ibid., p. 32.

98. Jung-pang Lo, "The decline", p. 152.

99. The same composition, almost word for word, is inscribed on the painting by which the court painters wished "to immortalize the extraordinary event", whose original Duyvendak had the good fortune to discover in 1939, together with a contemporary copy. (The original is now in the Chait Galleries in New York.) The inscription extolling the beauty and virtues of the giraffe states; "It has the the body of a deer and the tail of an ox, and a fleshy boneless horn, with luminous spots like a red cloud or a purple mist. Its hoofs do not tread on [living] beings and in its wanderings it carefully selects the ground. It walks in stately fashion and in its every motion it observes a rhythm. Its harmonious voice sounds like a bell or a musical tube." (Duyvendak, *China's Discovery*, p. 34.)

100. Duyvendak *China's Discovery*, p. 35.

101. Italiaander, p. 189.

102. Davidson, pp. 158–9.

103. Duyvendak, "The true dates", pp. 378–81.

104. Jung-pang Lo, "The emergence", p. 494, footnote 21.

105. Ibid., p. 503.

106. Jung-pang Lo, "The decline", pp. 150–1, and "The emergence", pp. 495–7. Jung-pang Lo says that during the Middle Ages changes in the climate and soil conditions of north-west China resulted in an impoverishment of that region, whilst at the same time there was a great economic advance in the south-eastern coastal region, which became the nation's economic centre. The establishment by foreign conquerors of strong militarist states in the north-west finally cut China's contacts with Central Asia, obliging it to conduct its cultural and commercial exchanges with the outside world by sea. Before the fall of K'ai-feng in 1127, 35 per cent of the tribute coming from tribute-with-trade missions came to China by land and 65 per cent by sea; after that date all came by sea (p. 497).

107. Jung-pang Lo, "The decline", p. 150. There were eight classes of warships, four being combat vessels and four reconnaissance craft (p. 150, footnote 2). Mills (p. 11) says that Ch'êng Tsu, continuing the policy of Kublai Khan, "attempted a thalassocracy of the Asiatic Seas".

108. "Cheng Ho hsia hsi-yang tu ch'uan" ("The ships of Cheng Ho's voyage to the Western Ocean"), T'ung-fang tsa-chih, 43, 1, January 1947, 48. A liao was about 500 pounds. For ships of 500 tons the dimensions given in various Ming works, of 444 feet long by 180 feet wide, seem disproportionate.

On the extraordinary development of the Chinese navy and merchant fleet not all authorities are in agreement. Thus Kuwabara (p. 70, footnote 31) says that the great expansion in naval construction under the Yüan ceased with the end of the Mongol dynasty; he quoted Professor Yano ("The opening of China", Shigaku Zasshi, May 1922): "During the Ming era, though we have read of marine adventures, such as the expedition of Chêng Ho to the Southern Seas, the government made it its principal object to guard the coasts and forbade the Chinese to communicate with the foreigners or to go abroad, observing the hereditary teaching that no ship whatever should be allowed to go to sea. This must have had a detrimental influence on the development of Chinese ships." It is clear, however, that both Kuwabara and Yano are referring to the isolationist policy started after 1435 by the Ming emperors, disregarding the successful expansionist policy of the early Ming period.

109. See Ming-shih, 322: 11 and 17, and 344: 25. See also T'ung Shu-yeh, pp. 239–46; Jung-pang Lo, "The decline", p. 154, footnote; Duyvendak, China's Discovery, p. 17.

110. Jung-pang Lo, "The decline", p. 154.

111. On his last voyage, in 1431, Cheng Ho was given 100,000 strings in banknotes to distribute in foreign countries.

112. Jung-pang Lo, "The decline,' p. 156.

113. Duyvendak, China's Discovery, p. 27.

114. Cheng Ho's travelling companions of at least his seventh voyage (according to Pelliot), Ma Huan, Fei Hsin and Kung Chen, collaborated on his biography, which is contained in the Ming-shih and has been translated by Greeneveldt in his "Notes on the Malay Archipelago, 41–45" (see Rockhill and Hirth, p. 81). The tomb of Cheng Ho is traditionally shown at Nanking, as Gaillard remarks in "Nankin, Aperçu historique, 199".

115. Duyvendak, China's Discovery, pp. 27–8.

116. See Hucker, Rideout, Mote and Crawford.

117. Duyvendak, China's Discovery, pp. 28 and 31, observes that Fei Hsin, author of the travel journal Hsin-ch'a sheng-lan, although a member of the scholar class, was doing compulsory military service on board ship in order to atone for some offence, perhaps of a political nature, committed

by his father or grandfather. The illustrated edition of his travel journal which was specially prepared for the Emperor was intended to win the good will of the Court and thus regain for him his liberty.

118. Jung-pang Lo, "The decline", p. 152.

119. Ibid., p. 164. For fuller accounts of the government organization of the Ming dynasty and the role of the eunuchs, see authors listed in reference 116 above. Hicker (pp. 11 and 24–5) notes that under the first Ming emperor the eunuchs were organized in a Directorate of Palace Assistants (*Nei-shih chien*); as they grew in number the Directorates expanded, and in the first half of the fifteenth century there were twelve of them (*chien*), with four Offices (*chü*). At the end of the century there were 10,000 eunuchs in the imperial palace alone, and in 1644 there were 70,000. Four famous enuchs who were something akin to real dictators followed each other during the course of almost two centuries—Wang (or Weng) Cheng in 1449, Wang Chih in 1470, Liu Chin around 1500, and finally the most celebrated of all, Wei Chung-hsien in 1620. Under them the normal functioning of the government was turned upside down and the supreme power fell into their hands.

120. See bibliography.

121. Needham (vol. III, pp. 558–61) writes that Cheng Ho's expeditions gave rise to four works of great importance written between 1434 and 1520, three of them compiled by men who were in his own retinue—Hung Chen and Fei Hsin (officers of the expeditionary corps) and Ma Huan, the Chinese Muslim interpreter. Needham is excluding Wang Ta–yüan's *Tao-i chih-lüeh* of 1349–50, and instead including Kung Chen's *Hsin-yang fan-kuo chih* of 1434. Pelliot ("Les grands voyages") dates three of these works differently as follows: (p. 260) *Tao-i chih-lüeh*, 1350; (pp. 218 and 264) *Ying yai sheng-lan*, between 1416 and 1451; *Hsi-yang fan-kuo chih*, 1434. In the second half of the seventeenth century Kung Chen's work was described by Ch'ien Tseng in his *Tu-shu min ch'iu chi*, which was later lost. Duyvendak ("Desultory notes", p. 5) considers that, since the accounts of foreign countries given in this work accord with those of the *Ming-shih*, it is probable that the compilers of the latter used it.

122. Rockhill and Hirth, pp. 622–6.

123. The first of the four works listed by Rockhill and Hirth, compiled a century before the next two and two centuries before the fourth.

124. Rockhill and Hirth, vol. XVI, pp. 72–3.

125. Davidson's bibliography erroneously gives Rockhill and Hirth's study as in vol. XV (1914) of *T'oung Pao*, whereas the descriptions of the East African coast are in vol. XVI (1915), pp. 614–18.

126. Some authors, like Rockhill and Hirth (vol. XVI, p. 616), have thought this a case of syllable inversion (La-sa = Sa-la). Herrmann (*Historical Atlas*) accepted this, but there is no firm evidence for the supposition. In the *Ming-shih* (326) La-sa is tentatively identified with Al-Ahsa. Duyvendak ("Desultory notes", pp. 20–7) says that Al-Ahsa or El Hasa is the name not of a city but of a coastal region on the north-west shores of the Persian Gulf. For Duyvendak the logical conclusion would be as follows: Al-Ahsa (La-sa) = Oman; the city would be Muscat. However, one cannot fail to point out that the Ming History (*Ming-shih*) speaking of La-sa says that "this country in all presented its tribute three times, and each time along with the countries of A-tan (Aden) and Pu-la-wa (Brava)" and that its buildings are in all respects similar to those of Chu-pu (Giumbo). This suggests a place rather on the Gulf of Aden (such as Zeila) than on the Persian Gulf. Kirkman, "The Culture of the Kenya Coast", p. 95, identifies La-sa with Mombasa.

127. Rockhill and Hirth, vol. XVI, pp. 614–15.
128. Ibid., p. 615. The identification of Chu-pu with Giumbo seems rather problematical, since Giumbo, near the mouth of the Juba, does not present the desolate appearance of the Chinese description. Grottanelli (pp. 63–70) suggests that it may refer to the section of the coast corresponding to "the Bajun country, rich in islands and about midway between Brava and Malindi".
129. Rockhill and Hirth, vol. XVI, pp. 617–18. Coupland (p. 37) writes: "Mogadishu figures also in the Chinese records of the Ming dynasty. The chronicler speaks slightingly of its barren, mountainous, and dry surroundings—'it sometimes does not rain for years'—but 'the houses', he says, 'are built of stone'. And it was Mogadishu that took the lead in the trade between East Africa and China which, to judge from the fragments of Ming ware found in the ruins of the coast towns, reached its zenith in the fourteenth or fifteenth century. In 1427 an envoy from Mogadishu was sent to China, and in 1430 a fleet of Chinese junks visited Mogadishu." The dates given by Coupland naturally do not correspond with those subsequently established by Sinologists on the basis of the two inscriptions of Cheng Ho.
130. Girace. On Girace's interpretation, Pirone (pp. 40–1) has much to say, and suggests that the reference to mountains concerns "probably [only] the higher dunes [of Mogadishu], like the so-called Fort Cecchi or the dunes of the Bondere quarter and the Arab village. . . . As regards the dryness of the land, the visit of the Chinese must have been after years of insufficient rainfall or prolonged dearth. After rains all the dunes around Mogadishu look quite different, covered with green and giving the visitor the idea of a smiling country rich in pasturage. . . . [Or] the descriptions of arid soil and unbroken mountains may have referred to the Migiurtinia region, as also the statement that the prime export product is incense. The salted fish eaten by the livestock could equally refer to the northern districts, where this has been noted during periods of prolonged drought. In the case of Brava and Giumbo there may have been confusion, perhaps because relying on second-hand information; or Fei Hsin and Cheng Ho himself may have made notes and only marshalled them on return home, making errors in the process."
131. See reference 117 above.
132. See note 51 above.
133. Duyvendak. "Voyages de Tcheng Houo", 5r–5v in the revised edition of Fei Hsin.
134. Ibid., Ming-shih, 326, 7v and 7v–8r.
135. Ibid., 8r–9r.
136. Ingrams, p. 88, and Schwarz, pp. 175 ff.
137. Pearce, pp. 49 and 344. Ingrams (p. 89) writes: "Idris remarks that, when great troubles arose in China, the Chinese transferred their trade to islands which he calls Zaledj or Zanedj, facing the coast of Zinj, where they came to intimate relations with the inhabitants on account of their mildness and accommodating ways." Grottanelli (p. 63) notes that "T'ang and Sung coins, of 7th–12th centuries, have been found in many coastal localities, including Kilwa, the Mafia islands, Zanzibar and Mogadishu".
138. Ingrams, p. 89.
139. Hirth, Ancient Porcelain.
140. Hirth, "Early Chinese notices", pp. 56–7.
141. See Freeman-Grenville's writings listed in the bibliography, and also his introductory note to Dr. Baumann's study on the island of Mafia in Tanganyika Notes and Records, No. 46, January 1957, p. 1, in which he

refers to the Chinese coins of the thirteenth–fifteenth centuries found at Kilwa.

142. No Chinese coins or porcelain are listed in the *Catalogo del Museo della Garesa*, ed. F. S. Caroselli, Regio Governo della Somalia, Mogadishu, 1934. The author has, however, ascertained that some Chinese coins and procelain fragments are to be found in private collections in Mogadishu.

143. Referring to Mogadishu coins, Freeman–Grenville ("Some problems") calls them "eight exceptions from the Mogadishu collection".

144. *T'oung Pao*, vol. XLVII, Books 1–2, 1959, "Mélanges", pp. 81–3. The author is grateful to Messrs. Brill and the Editors of the journal for permission to reproduce the accompanying plates.

145. Schwarz, p. 177.

146. Pearce, p. 357; Stigand, p. 155. Schwarz (p. 177) writes: "The whole coast from Kismayu to Zanzibar is littered with Chinese pottery, which Major Pearce had determined at the British Museum as dating from the Sung to the Ming dynasties, and his collection is now in the Museum in Zanzibar that bears his name."

147. Kirkman ("Excavations at Ras Mkumbuu", p. 169) writes: "A sherd of cream coloured porcelain, now in the Victoria and Albert Museum, was extracted from this cavity [near the base of the pillar]. It was described as Ting ware of the Sung dynasty, but I believe it to be similar to my G.GM 5 (Chinese White) which has been found frequently in fifteenth century levels in Kenya" (e.g. Gedi, Mnarani and Ungwana).

148. Church, p. 315; Fripp, NADA, No. 17, pp. 88–96 and No. 18, pp. 12–22; Schwarz, p. 182.

149. Pearce, p. 358.

150. Strandes, p. 88, footnote 1 (see reference 61 above).

151. Pearce, p. 359. Robinson (p. 85) writes: "Some of the bowls which have been removed are now in London and other museums where they are exhibited as examples of Chinese art. There is some doubt as to the Chinese origin of many of these bowls, some of which have been sold to collectors. It would appear that Chinese artisans made bowls of imitation Chinese porcelain and forged the ancient marks after copying the style."

152. Tanner.

153. There are also small but interesting collections of Chinese porcelain, in fairly good state of preservation, in the Coryndon Museum in Nairobi, in the Museum of Fort Jesus in Mombasa, and in the Museum at Gedi in Kenya.

154. Freeman-Grenville, "Chinese porcelain in Tanganyika", pp. 63–4.

155. Ibid. Presumably, Hunter (p. 137) is referring to the same two bowls when he writes: "The two bowls removed from the pillar of the tomb at Kaole are celadon wares from China and are of a type made in the 14th century and earlier. The bowl placed uppermost has a dark grey porcelanous-stoneware body covered with a grey-green glaze. The foot-ring is small and square-cut and without glaze inside, The second bowl is of similar design and proportions but has a light-grey and a smooth, subdued, sea-green glaze."

156. Freeman-Grenville, ibid. Robinson (p. 84) says: "In East Africa there was a common practice of affixing bowls of a Chinese type in the facades of tomb-mosques or on the head-posts of tombs." Hunter (p. 134) writes: "At one time many of the tombs were decorated with plates and bowls cemented into their structure, but these have been removed in the past leaving only two bowls set in the top of the tallest pillar."

157. Freeman-Grenville, ibid. He recalls that in the Middle Ages magic powers were attributed to porcelain. The Persian philosopher At-Tusi (1207–47),

in a work written for the edification of the Mongol Emperor Hulagu Khan, said that if a poisoned foodstuff was placed in a celadon bowl it would sweat, and also that celadon reduced to powder was an excellent toothpaste and a specific for nose-bleeding. Tanner (pp. 83–4) says: "It is interesting to remember that another reason for the popularity of the celadon pottery was the fact that it had a reputed power of detecting poison in anything placed in it."

158. Kirkman, "Excavations at Ras Mkumbuu", pp. 171–2, described the porcelain findings, with drawings.

159. Ibid., p. 173.

160. Kirkman, "The culture of the Kenya Coast" and "Historical archaeology in Kenya".

161. Kirkman, "The culture", p. 89.

162. Ibid., p. 92.

163. Kirkman, "Historical archaeology", p. 22, and "The culture of the Kenya Coast", p. 95: "The economic activities that had brought the porcelain to Africa continued to grow in volume accelerated by the prosperity of the Ming Dynasty in China, and its demand for ivory, which could only now be obtained from Africa. A fleet of Chinese junks often visited MA-LIN-DI and LA-SA (Mombasa) between AD 1417 and 1419. . . . The reason for such an unprecedented feat can be found in the restless and grandiloquent character of the Emperor Yung-lo, influenced by the eunuch Cheng Tok (originally known as Haji Ma, a Moslem and a foreigner) whose position would naturally be exalted by the Emperor's interest in the countries of the west." For Kirkman's identification of La-Sa, see reference 126 above.

164. Kirkman, "The excavations at Kilepwa" and "The great pillars".

165. Kirkman, "Mnarani of Kilifi".

166. Kirkman, "The tomb of the dated inscription".

167. Mathew, "Songo Mnara", p. 159, writes: "Since I sent in my Report to the Tanganyika Government, Dr. William Cohn has identified three shards that I found on site A as Yüan were and has suggested that one of them might even be late Sung. But there is nothing surprising in good 13th century celadon on a 14th century site; fine ware would normally stay in circulation well over a century. The mass of the shards seemed Early or Middle Ming." Mathew also states ("Recent discoveries", p. 212) that during the preliminary digs in the abandoned city of the coral island of Songo Mnara he was able to examine and identify a large quantity of Chinese porcelain which was dated to the end of the Sung period and the beginning of the Ming period. A reference to celadon finds in Songo Mnara island is also to be found in *Annual Report of the Antiquities Division for the year 1960*, Tanganyika Ministry of Education, Dar-es-Salaam, 1962, p. 11.

168. Chittick (p. 184) described this important find as follows: "The glaze is blue-green, crackled. The base has been made in two parts: first the ring and sides of the vessel, into which a glazed bowl has been inserted from the inside, and cemented to the outer portion by its own glaze in firing. The foot-ring is unglazed and burnt red."

169. *Annual Report of the Department of Antiquities for 1958*, Dar-es-Salaam, 1959, p. 18.

170. Ditto for 1959, Dar-es-Salaam, 1960, p. 11.

171. *Annual Report of the Antiquities Division for 1960*, Dar-es-Salaam, 1962, pp. 3, 10 and 12.

172. Bretschneider (*On the Knowledge Possessed*) was one of the first European scholars to carry out detailed research into Chinese trade with the Arabs in the Middle Ages. See esp. pp. 13–22.

173. Curle, pp. 320-1. Shinnie refers to the discovery of fragments of Chinese porcelain, mostly celadon, in Socotra, datable in his opinion to the sixteenth-seventeenth centuries.

174. Grottanelli, p. 63. The fragments of Chinese porcelain which Grottanelli sent to the Museum of Ceramics in Faenza for identification are listed in an appendix (pp. 389–90). These small pieces were found as follows: nos. 2 and 3 at Ciula, nos. 4 and 8 at Ngumi, nos. 5, 6 and 9 at Ciovayi, and no. 7 at Rasini.

175. Mathew ("Recent discoveries", p. 217) says of the King George V Memorial Museum in Dar-es-Salaam that its very interesting collection of coins and porcelain fragments is unfortunately lacking in the documentation necessary for establishing their identity and provenance.

176. According to Schwarz (p. 181) the Ming pottery found in the Zimbabwe ruins does not prove that the Chinese were ever in that place, since such products could be easily imported. As regards Inyanga and Usambara, much could be established by systematic excavations. As regards the coast, however, the enormous quantity of finds make it unmistakably clear that the Chinese junks plied here in fairly remote times, since these are not modern pieces but authentic Sung pottery of extreme rarity. Fripp ("A note", p. 88) recalls how Maciver and Miss Caton Thompson found medieval Chinese porcelain on these sites, and that he was himself present when among a group of ruins in January 1939 porcelain was found on the surface, evidently the result of recent heavy rains; this consisted of fragments of celadon and a fine black-glazed ware later identified as Honan and dated not earlier than the thirteenth century.

177. Cerulli, *Somalia*, vol. I, "Nuovi documenti arabi per la storia di Mogadiscio", pp. 25–40, Caniglia also mentions "Ammar-Giageb".

178. Pirone, p. 38.

179. Pelliot, "Les grands voyages".

180. The tablet was inscribed in Chinese, Tamil and Persian, in honour of the local Buddha, to whom was attributed the power of keeping these waters safe. See Duyvendak, *China's Discovery*, pp. 29–30: "It is an interesting example of the universality of Chinese religious ideas that Cheng Ho, himself a Mohammedan, should be delegated to perform these sacrifices by Imperial command in the one case to a local divinity of south China, in the other to a Buddhistic divinity [of] Ceylon."

181. Pelliot, op. cit., p. 241.

182. Sinologists in general agree on the number of the ships and their complements in Cheng Ho's expeditions. Reservations have been expressed about the size and burden of the vessels and the composition of their crews, as given by Western travellers such as Marco Polo, Odorico da Pordenone and Ibn Battuta. The junks have been described as very wide vessels, almost square in shape, but with a narrow keel; they were armed against pirates (see Duyvendak, *China's Discovery*, p. 18, and reference 108 above).

183. Pelliot, "Les Grands voyages", pp. 273 ff.

184. The dates given for the presentation of the giraffe at Court do not agree (1414, 1415, 1416 ?), partly because, as has been noted, the tribute of this animal must have been repeated more than once (see references 96 and 102 above).

185. Pelliot, op. cit., pp. 198–9. See also reference 126 above.

186. The dates and routes given for these six voyages of Cheng Ho do not correspond to those given in his inscriptions, which were found after Pelliot was writing.

187. Pelliot, op. cit., p. 448.

188. *Ming-shih*, 8, 1–b.

189. The edict carried the date of 19th June 1430, but another preliminary edict must have been promulgated on 25th May 1430.

190. *Ming-shih*, 304, 2–a.

191. See reference 121 above.

192. Pelliot, op. cit., pp. 67–8.

193. "In 1431–3, between the ships under Cheng Ho's own command and those detached from his fleet, the whole Indian Ocean was traversed." Pelliot considers that this is unmistakably confirmed by a document translated by Mayers, pp. 329–30.

194. Duvendak, *China's Discovery* and "Voyages de Tcheng Houo" and "The true dates".

195. See also Duyvendak, "Ma Huan re-examined". Philips, "The seaports", gives as an appendix the map contained in the edition of *Wu-pei-chih* published shortly after 1628. Philips, pp. 221–4 identifies the names on the map as follows: 25, Ma-lin-ti, Malindi; 29, Man-pa-sa, Mombasa; 38, Pu-la-wa, Brava; 39, Mu-ku-tou-su, Mogadishu; 43, Hei-êrh, The Blacks, Sofala; 44, Ha-pu-ni (misprint, probably Ha-pu-hsi), the Arabic Habash, Abyssinia; 60, Hsü-to-ta-hsü, called by foreigners Su-ku-ta-la, the island of Socotra.

An idea of the countries known to the Chinese from remote times, and of the routes followed by Arab merchants trading to China and from China westwards, can be obtained from the map appended by Hirth and Rockhill to *Chau Ju-kua*, and from Herrmann's *Historical and Commercial Atlas of China*. The latter shows how the fleet, sailing from Hormuz, coasting along Oman and the Hadramawt, touched Aden and Zeila and rounded Cape Guardafui, reaching Mogadishu, Brava and Giumbo. For another map showing the trade routes of the Indian Ocean in the fifteenth century, see Oliver, ed., "The Dawn of African History", p. 49 (fig. 16).

196. This is evidently an error in transcription by the contemporary copyist—3,000 instead of 30, the figure which is given in the rest of the second inscription.

197. The miraculous light referred to by Cheng Ho must be the "St Elmo's fires", a natural phenomenon well known to seamen. Duyvendak (p. 29) writes: "To this miracle, which occurred on the first voyage, we owe the erection of the two tablets and with these the preservation of the true dates of the expeditions!"

198. Duyvendak, "The true dates", pp. 345–7.

199. There is disagreement both on the dates and on the routes of Cheng Ho's expeditions. Pelliot has the fleet putting in at the Somali coast both on the fourth and on the fifth voyage, and also on the seventh. Cheng Ho's inscriptions speak unmistakably of the Somali coast for the fifth voyage only, but leave it to be understood for the sixth. The destinations of the seventh expedition, then starting, are of course not mentioned.

200. Duyvendak identifies the *mi-li-kao* (*T'oung Pao*, vol. XXXV, 1939, pp. 211–15) with the "nilgau" or "nilg(h)ai", *Boscephalus tragocamelus*, a specimen of Indian antelope.

201. Duyvendak, "The true dates", pp. 349–55.

202. Duyvendak, "The true dates", p. 392, quotes a passage of the *Shu-yuan Tsa-chi* (1466): "During our dynasty the troops were composed of banished criminals. Their sons and grandsons from generation to generation were made to remain in the military service. This was called the Perennial Army." The *Ming-shih* (chap. 93, p. 11*b*) writes: "When a person is eighty years old or more or when he is gravely ill and commits a crime for which he

should be condemned to permanent military service [on the frontier], his son or his grandson can be exiled in his place."

203. The first inscription gives the year of the fourth voyage as the twelfth year of Yung-lo, while the second gives it as the eleventh year. The stone original of the second was found, while the first is only a copy; Duyvendak considers that the "11th year" of the first inscription is certainly a copyist's error.

204. The first inscription gives the fifth year of Hsüan-tê for the departure for Cheng Ho's last voyage, and the second inscription gives the sixth year. In this case the discrepancy is easily explicable if one considers the ten months that elapsed between the assembly of the fleet at Liu-chia-chiang and its actual departure from Ch'ang-lo as soon as the north wind began to blow. However, although the discovery of the two inscriptions has more or less finally cleared up some uncertainties and filled some gaps in knowledge, Sinologists have come on new problems of interpretation and consistency, above all regarding the basic Chinese manuscripts. See Duyvendak, "The true dates", pp. 355 ff.

205. Cordier, vol. III, p. 33.

206. Pelliot, "Les grands voyages", p. 238.

207. Reusch, p. 153.

208. Ingrams writes (p. 95): "In these days, then, especially those of the Ming dynasty, Chinese shipping reached far over the seas, and they had considerable overseas trade; as this was so, and as their descendants are still trading here today, it may be wondered why they have not developed their sea trade more. Mr. Wells has admirably summed up the reasons in his *Outline of History* and traces them without doubt to the difficulties of writing, speaking and learning Chinese, which even to this day makes Chinese history and the general study of China a closed book to all but the few. Such a drawback cannot but have acted adversely on their relations with Bantu peoples. Other languages they could, and did assimilate, but Chinese would offer almost insuperable difficulties." See also Schwarz, p. 181.

209. Duyvendak found this ordinance in the *T'ai-ts'ang chou-chih* (1919 edition, chap. 13, 3b). The *Shih-lu* also says that in 1433 embassies arrived from the Western countries (Arabia is named, but not East Africa) with tributes of giraffes, elephants, horses, etc. To the Minister of the Rites and other functionaries who came to congratulate him, the Emperor sternly replied: "The products of distant countries cause me no emotion. What I consider is the absolute sincerity with which the ambassadors have brought them, and it is only for this that I receive them. There is no need to congratulate me." It seems that the ambassadors, however, stayed in China from 1433 to 1436.

210. Duyvendak, "The true dates", p. 395.

211. Cheng Ho's ventures prompted some fantastic narrations, in which the inspiration of Dante's *Divina Commedia* is evident. In the last part of a singular work entitled *San-Pao t'ai-chien hsia hsi-yang chi*, written in 1597 by Lo Mou-teng, one finds the fullest account in Chinese of a journey to the beyond. The initial narrative is a highly romanticized description of "the historic voyages undertaken between 1405 and 1432 in the countries of the sea of southern China and the India Ocean, under the command of the Eunuch Cheng Ho". The narrator imagines that the whole expedition (which was accompanied by the Taoist T'ien-shih or "Patron of Heaven" and by the Buddhist Kuo-shih) visited Mecca (in fact some members of Chieng Ho had actually done so). Here the admiral asked about the existence of other countries still further west, and being told there was none, nevertheless insisted on continuing his explorations even if they should lead him

into the realm of the underworld. At this point the fantastic journey commences. Having sailed to a country without sun and without stars, the admiral sent ashore an official named Wang Ming to explore the land. The setting of the subsequent episodes and their characters clearly recalls Dante's Inferno and Purgatorio (see Duyvendak, "A Chinese 'Divina Commedia' ").

212. Duyvendak (p. 27) writes: "It is said that about 1480 another eunuch who had risen to great power, wished to imitate Chêng Ho and start a maritime expedition against Annam. For this purpose he asked for the official records of Chêng Ho's expeditions. With the connivance of the high officials of the War Office these records were thereupon destroyed, so as to frustrate the eunuch's attempts to organize an expedition."

213. San Pao, as noted above, was the title by which Cheng Ho was generally known.

214. Duyvendak, "The true dates", pp. 395–6. Italiaander (p. 189) says that "those who took part in the expeditions were forbidden to speak about them, and even the reports and charts of the voyages disappeared from the imperial archives—presumably consigned to the flames".

215. For the value of a tael, see reference 77.

216. Jung-pang Lo, "The decline", p. 153.

217. Ibid., p. 167, and Duyvendak, "China's Discovery", p. 28.

218. Jung-pang Lo, ibid.

219. Jung-pang Lo, "The emergence", pp. 494–5 and footnote 21.

220. Jung-pang Lo, "The decline", pp. 164–5.

221. Goodrich, "A note on Professor Duyvendak's lectures". The mission sent by Egypt to China in 1441 is also referred to by Bretschneider (*Mediaeval Researches*) and by Pelliot ("Les anciens rapports"). The Ming History also states that on the tenth moon of the sixth year, or 15th October 1441, the envoy of Mi-hsi-êrh (Misr, or Egypt), Su-wu Pa-tu-êrh (Suwu Bahadur ?) stated that the ruler of T'ien-fang (Arabia) had sent his own son Sai-i-tê A-li (Sayyid Ali) with the ambassador Sai-i-tê Ha-san (Sayyid Hasan) to bring products of his region and present them as tribute. When they reached the country of Ha-la (Karakhojo) they were attacked by robbers; Sai-i-tê Ha-san was killed and Sai-i-tê A-li was injured in one hand, and the tribute, clothing and baggage were stolen. The Emperor ordered the Ministers of Ceremonial and of War to draw up an inventory of the stolen property and to report to him.

122. Jung-pang Lo, "The decline", pp. 156–7.

223. Ibid., pp. 158–68.

224. Grottanelli, pp. 63–70 and illustration 255, p. 81. Italiaander (p. 188) speaks of the existence in Kenya of "a number of Asian families, certainly of Chinese origin, established a long time since". See also Elliot.

G

Bibliography

Annual Report of the Department of Antiquities for the Year 1958, Government Printer, Tanganyika, Dar es Salaam, 1959, 49 pp.

Annual Report of the Department of Antiquities for the Year 1959, idem, 1960, 16 pp.

Annual Report of the Antiquities Division for the Year 1960, Ministry of Education, Tanganyika, Government Printer, Dar es Salaam, 1962, 21 pp.

Audemard, L. Les Jonques Chinoises, I: Histoire de la Jonque, Rotterdam, Museum voor Land en Volkenkunde en Maritiem Museum "Prins Hendrik", 1957, 97 pp. with illustrations and a map.

Battuta, Ibn. Travels in Asia and Africa, 1325–54, tr. H. A. R. Gibb, London, 1929.

——Voyages d'Ibn Batoutah. Arabic text with translation by C. Defrémery and B. R. Sanguinetti, 4 vols., Société Asiatique de Paris, 1958. A translation of Ibn Battuta's work into Italian by Professor F. Gabrieli has been published by Sansoni.

Bretschneider, E. On the Knowledge Possessed by the Ancient Chinese of the Arabs and Arabian Colonies, London, 1871, 18 pp.

——"Chinese intercourse with the countries of Central and Eastern Asia", Journal of the North China Branch of the Royal Asiatic Society, 1876.

——Mediaeval Researches from Eastern Asiatic Sources, 2 vols., 1888.

Caniglia, G. "Note storiche sulla città di Mogadiscio", Rivista Coloniale, Rome, 12th Year, 30 April 1917, pp. 172–88.

Cerulli, E. Somalia: Scritti vari editi e inediti, Amministrazione Fiduciaria Italiana della Somalia, 2 vols., Rome, 1957 and 1959.

Chatterton, E. Keble. Sailing Ships and Their Story, London, 1909.

Chavannes, ed. "Les Deux plus anciens spécimens de la cartographie chinoise", extract from Bulletin de l'École Française d'Extrême Orient, Hanoi, Schneider, 1903, 35 pp. with reproductions of the two Chinese maps.

——"Les pays d'occident d'après le Weï-lio", extract from T'oung Pao, series II, vol. VIII, no. 2, 1907, 88 pp. with 19 tables of the Chinese text.

Chittick, H. N. "Notes on Kilwa", Tanganyika Notes and Records, Dar-es-Salaam, no. 53, October 1959, pp. 179–203.

——A Guide to the Ruins of Kilwa, with Some Notes on other Antiquities in the Region, Dar es Salaam, National Culture and Antiquities Division, Ministry of Community Development and National Culture, 1965, 23 pp.

——"Discoveries in the Lamu Archipelago", extract from Azania, vol. II, 1967, 31 pp.

Chou Shih-te. "Notes on the great ships of Cheng Ho: A discussion based on a study of the tiller found at the side of a Ming dynasty shipyard", Wen Wu (Peking), 1962–63, pp. 35–30.

Church, Major A. East Africa, a New Dominion, London, Witherby, 1927.

Cordier, H. Histoire Générale de la Chine et de ses relations avec les pays étrangers, 4 vols., Paris, Paul Geuthner, 1920–21.

Cornevin, R. Histoire des peuples de l'Afrique Noire, Paris, Berger-Levrault, 1960.

——Histoire de l'Afrique, vol. I: Des origines au XVIe siècle, Paris, Payot, 1962.

Coupland, R. East Africa and its Invaders, Oxford, Clarendon Press, 1938.

Crawford, R. B. "Eunuch power in the Ming dynasty", T'oung Pao, vol. XLIX, 1961, pp. 115–48.

Crone, G. R. "Fra Mauro's representation of the Indian Ocean and the Eastern Islands", Studi Colombani (Genoa), vol. III, 1951.

Curle, A. T. "The ruined cities of Somaliland", *Antiquity*, vol. XI, September. 1937, pp. 315–27.

Darrag, Ahmed. *L'Égypte dans le règne de Barsbay 825–41/1422–38*, Damascus, Institut Français de Damas, 1961. Chapters include (pp. 195–201) "Les routes du commerce avec l'Extrême-Orient au début du XV siècle", and (pp. 217–21) "Relations diplomatiques avec l'Inde et la Chine".

Dart, A. R. "A Chinese character as a wall motive in Rhodesia", *South African Journal of Science*, vol. XXXVI, December 1939 (1940), pp. 474–6, with illustration.

Davidson, B. *Old Africa Rediscovered*, London, Gollancz, 1960.

Deschamps, H. *Histoire de Madagascar*, Paris, Berger-Levrault, 1961.

Dracopoli, I. N. *Through Jubaland to the Lorian Swamp*, London, Steeley, 1914.

Duyvendak, J. J. L. *Ma Huan Reexamined*, Verhandelingen van de Koninklijke Akademie van Wetenschappen te Amsterdam, Afd. Letterkunde, Nieuwe Reeks, Deel XXXII, no. 2, Amsterdam, 1933.

——"Sailing directions of Chinese voyages", *T'oung Pao*, vol. XXXIV, 1938, pp. 230–7.

——"The true dates of the Chinese maritime expeditions in the early fifteenth century", *T'oung Pao*, vol. XXXIV, 1938, pp. 341–412.

——"Voyages de Tcheng Houo à la côte orientale d'Afrique, 1416 à 1443", in Youssuf Kemal, *Extrait des Monumenta cartographica Africae et Aegypti*, vol. IV, fasc. 4, Leyden, Brill, 1939.

——*China's Discovery of Africa*, Lectures given at the University of London on 22nd and 23rd January 1947, London, Probsthain, 1949, 35 pp., illustrations.

——"Desultory notes on the *Hsi-yang-chi*", *T'oung Pao*, vol. XLII, 1953, Books 1–2, pp. 1–35.

——"A Chinese *Divina Commedia*", *T'oung Pao*, vol. XLI, 1953, Books 4–5, pp. 255–316.

Elliot, J. A. G. "A visit to the Bajun islands", *Journal of the British African Society*, vol. XXV, 1926, nos. 97–100, 74 pp.

Eldridge, F. B. *The Background of Eastern Sea Power*, Melbourne, 1948.

Fa, Hsien, *Travels (399–414 A.D.), or Record of the Buddhistic Kingdoms*, tr. H. A. Giles, London, 1923.

Fairbank, J. K. and Reischauer, E. O. *East Asia: The Great Tradition*, Boston, 1960.

Fairgrieve, J. *Geography and World Power*, London, 1921.

Ferrand, Gabriel. *Relation des voyages et textes géographiques arabes, persans, turcs*, Paris, 1914.

Foster, N. "A note on some ruins near Bagamoyo", *Tanganyika Notes and Records*, no. 3, pp. 106 ff.

Franke, O. *Geschichte des Chinesischen Reiches: Eine Darstellung seiner Entstehung, seines Wesens und seiner Entwicklung bis zur neuesten Zeit*, Berlin, Walter de Gruyer, vols. IV and V, 1948 and 1952.

Freeman-Grenville, G. S. P. "Chinese porcelain in Tanganyika", *Tanganyika Notes and Records*, no. 41, December 1955, pp. 63–6.

——"Coinage in East Africa before Portuguese times", *Numismatic Chronicle*, 1957.

——"Some problems of East African coinages: From early times to 1890", *Tanganyika Notes and Records*, no. 53, October 1959, pp. 259–60.

——"East African coin finds and their historical significance", *Journal of African History*, vol. I, 1960, no. 1, pp. 31–43.

Fripp, C. E. "A note on Mediaeval Chinese-African trade", *Native Affairs Department Annual* (Salisbury), no. 17, 1940, pp. 88–96.

Fripp, C. E. "Chinese Mediaeval trade with Africa", *Native Affairs Department Annual* (Salisbury), no. 18, 1941, pp. 12–22.

Fuchs, W. "Was South Africa known in the 13th century?", *Imago Mundi*, X, 1950, p. 50 (with Chinese–Korean map of Ch'üon Chin, 1402).

Girace, A. "Le costa della Somalia e i Cinesi", *Corriere della Somalia* (Mogadishu), no. 207, 2nd September 1954.

Goodrich, L. C. "Negroes in China", *Bulletin of the Catholic University of Peking* (Peking), 1931, pp. 137–8.

——"A note on Professor Duyvendak's lectures on China's discovery of Africa", *Bulletin of the School of Oriental and African Studies*, vol. XIV, part II, 1952, pp. 384–7.

——"The connection between the nautical charts of the Arabs and those of the Chinese before the days of the Portuguese navigations", *I.S.I.S.*, vol. XLIV, 1953, pp. 99–100.

——"Recent discoveries at Zeyton", *Journal of the American Oriental Society* (Baltimore), no. 77, 1957, pp. 161 ff.

Gray, B. *Early Chinese Pottery and Porcelain*, London, 1953.

Grottanelli, V. L. *Pescatori dell'Oceano Indiano*, Rome, Cremonese, 1955.

Hennig, R. "Ein Arabischer Schiff am Kap der Guten Hoffnung und im südlichen Ozean um 1420", *Terrae Incognitae*, 2nd edn., vol. IV, 1956, pp. 44–5.

——"Eine Chinesische Gesandschaftsreise nach Arabien (1422)", *Terrae Incognitae*, 2nd edn., vol. IV, 1956, pp. 56–60.

Herrmann, A. *Ein Seeverkehr zwischen Abessinien and Süd-China zu Beginn unserer Zeitrechnung*, Berlin, Zeitschrift der Berliner Gesellschaft für Erdkunde, 1913, 553 pp.

——*Die Verkehrswege zwischen China, Indien und Rom um etwa 100 nach Chr.*, Leipzig, 1922.

——*Historical and Commercial Atlas of China*, Harvard, 1935.

Hirth, F. *China and the Roman Orient*, Shanghai, Helly and Walsh; Leipzig and Munich, G. Hirth, 1885.

——*Ancient Porcelain: A Study in Chinese Mediaeval Industry and Trade*, Leipzig, 1888. Contains a mention of the visit of a Chinese fleet (clearly Cheng Ho's) to Mogadishu in 1430.

——"Early Chinese notices of East African territories", *Journal of the American Oriental Society* (New Haven, Connecticut), vol. XXX, 1909–10, pp. 46 ff.

——"The story of Chang K'ien, China's pioneer in Western Asia" (text and translation of Chapter 123 of Ssi-ma Ts'ien's *Shĭ-ki*), *Journal of the American Oriental Society* (New Haven, Connecticut), vol. XXXVII, part 2, September 1917, pp. 89–152.

Hirth, F. and Rockhill, W. W. *Chau Ju-kua: His Work on the Chinese and Arab Trade in the Twelfth and Thirteenth Centuries, Entitled "Chu-fan-chï"*, translated and annotated, St. Petersburg, Printing Office of the Imperial Academy of Sciences, 1912, 288 pp., with map illustrating the "Description of the barbarian peoples".

Hollingsworth, L. W. *A Short History of the East Coast of Africa*, London, Macmillan 1960 (first edition 1929).

Howorth, Sir H. H. "Buddhism in the Pacific", *Journal of the Royal Anthropological Institute*, vol. LI, 1921.

Hsiang Ta. "A great Chinese navigator", *China Reconstructs*, July 1956, pp. 11–14.

Hucker, C. O. "Governmental organizations of the Ming dynasty", *Harvard Journal of Asiatic Studies*, vol. XXI, December 1958, pp. 1–66.

Hudson, G. F. *Europe and China: A Survey of Their Relations from the Earliest Times to 1800*, London, Arnold, 1931.

Hunter, G. A. "A note on some tombs at Kaole", *Tanganyika Notes and Records*, no. 37, July 1954, pp. 134–7.

Ingham, K. A. *A History of East Africa*, London, Longmans, 1962.

Ingrams, W. H. *Zanzibar, Its History and People*, London, Witherby, 1931.

Italiaander, R. *Der ruhelose Kontinent*, Dusseldorf, Econ-Verlag, 1961.

Kirkman, J. "The excavations at Kilepwa", *Antiquaries' Journal*, vol. XXXII, July–October 1952, pp. 168–84.

——"The Arab city of Gedi: Excavations at the Great Mosque", *Architecture and Finds* (Oxford), 1954.

——"Ruined cities of Azania", *Outlook* (Johannesburg), vol. XI, no. 3.

——"The culture of the Kenya coast in the later Middle Ages: Some conclusions from excavations 1948–56", *South African Archaeological Bulletin*, vol. XI, no. 44, December 1956, pp. 89–99.

——"Takwa: The Mosque of the Pillar", *Ars Orientalis II*, 1957.

——"Historical archaeology in Kenya", *Antiquaries' Journal*, vol. XXXVII, January–April 1957, pp. 16–28.

——"The great pillars of Malindi and Mambrui", *Oriental Art*, new series, vol. IV, 1958, pp. 56–67.

——"Excavations at Ras Mkumbuu on the island of Pemba", *Tanganyika Notes and Records*, no. 53, 1959, pp. 161–78.

——"Mnarani of Kilifi: The mosques and tombs", *Ars Orientalis III*, 1959, pp. 96–112.

——"The tomb of the dated inscription at Gedi", Royal Anthropological Institute, *Occasional Paper* no. 14, 1960.

——*Guide to Fort Jesus, Mombasa*, Mombasa, 1960.

——*Gedi: The Palace*, The Hague, 1962.

Kuwabara, J. "On P'u Shou-kêng, a man of the Western Regions who was Superintendent of the Trading Ships' Office in Ch'üan-chou towards the end of the Sung Dynasty, together with a general sketch of trade of the Arabs in China during the T'ang and Sung Eras", *Memoirs of the Research Department of the Toyo Bunko* (The Oriental Library, Tokyo), 1928, pp. 1–79.

Laufer, B. "Arabic and Chinese trade in walrus and narwhal ivory", *T'oung Pao*, vol. XIV, 1913, p. 323.

Lo, Jung-pang. "The emergence of China as a sea power during the late Sung and early Yüan periods", *Far Eastern Quarterly*, vol. XIV, no. 4, August 1955, pp. 489–504.

——"The decline of the early Ming navy", *Oriens Extremus* (Hamburg), vol. V, December 1958, pp. 149–68.

Mahler, G. J. *The Westerners among the Figurines of the T'ang Dynasty of China*, Rome, Istituto per il Medio ed Estremo Oriente, 1959.

Marsh, Z. A. and Kingsworth, G. *An Introduction to the History of East Africa*, Cambridge University Press, 1957.

Mathew, G. "Chinese porcelain in East Africa and on the coast of Arabia", *Oriental Art*, new series, vol. II, no. 2, 1956.

——"Songo Mnara", *Tanganyika Notes and Records*, no. 63, October 1959, pp. 155–60.

——"Recent discoveries in East African archaeology", *Antiquity*, vol. XXVII, 1953, no. 108, pp. 212–18.

Mayers, W. F. "Chinese explorations of the Indian Ocean during the XV century", *China Review*, vol. III, 1874, pp. 219–331; vol. IV, 1875, pp. 61 ff.

Mills, J. V. "Notes on early Chinese voyages", *Journal of the Royal Asiatic Society*, 1951, parts I and II, pp. 3–25.

Mote, F. W. "The growth of Chinese despotism: A critique of Wittfogel's theory of oriental despotism as applied to China", *Oriens Extremus* (Hamburg), vol. VIII, 1961, pp. 1–41.

Needham, J. *Science and Civilization in China*, vol. I, *Introductory Orientations*, Cambridge University Press, 1954; vol. II, *History of Scientific Thought*, 1956; vol. III, *Mathematics and the Sciences of the Heavens and the Earth*, 1959; vol. IV, part I, *Mechanical Engineering*, 1965; vol. IV, part II, *Civil Engineering and Nautics*, 1971.

Oliver, R. and Fage, J. D. *A Short History of Africa*, Penguin Books, 1962.

Oliver, R., ed. *The Dawn of African History*, Oxford University Press, 1961.

Pao Tsun-p'eng. "The ships used by Cheng Ho on his voyages to the West", *Hsin-ya hsüeh-pao* (New Asia Journal), Hong Kong, vol. IV, 1960, no. 2, pp. 307–51.

Pearce, Major F. B. *Zanzibar: The Island Metropolis of East Africa*, London, Fisher Unwin, 1920.

Pelliot, P. Review of Hirth and Rockhill's *Chau Ju-kua*, *T'oung Pao*, vol. XIII, July 1912, no. 3, pp. 466–81.

——"Les anciens rapports entre l'Égypte et l'Extrême-Orient", Proceedings of *Congrès International de Gèographie*, vol. V, 1926, pp. 21 ff.

——"Les grands voyages maritimes chinois au début du XV siècle, *T'oung Pao*, vol. XXX, 1933, nos. 3–5, pp. 237–452.

——"Notes additonelles sur Tcheng Houo et sur ses voyages", *T'oung Pao*, vol. XXXI, 1934–35, pp. 274–314.

——"Encore à propos des voyages de Tcheng Houo", *T'oung Pao*, vol. XXXII, 1936, pp. 210–22.

——i*Notes on Marco Polo*, Paris, Imprimerie Nationale, 1959.

Philips, G. "The seaports of India and Ceylon", *Journal of the China Branch of the Royal Asiatic Society*, new series, vol. XX, 1885, pp, 209 ff.

——"Précis translations of the *Ying yai shêng lan*", *Journal of the Royal Asiatic Society*, 1895, p. 529, and 1896, p. 341.

Pirenne, J. "Un problème-clef pour la chronologie de l'Orient: La date du Périple de la Mer Erythrée", *Journal Asiatique*, CCXLIX, 1961, pp. 441–59.

Pirone, M. *Appunti di Storia dell'Africa II: Somalia*, Istituto Universitario della Somalia, Rome, "Ricerche", 1961.

Polo, Marco. Sir Henry Yule's edition, *The Book of Ser Marco Polo the Venetian*, ed. H. Cordier, London, Murray, 1921.

——*Il Milione*, ed. L. Benedetto, Florence, Olschki, 1928. (Benedetto's text was translated into English in the "Broadway Travellers" series in 1931.)

——*The Description of the World*, ed. A. C. Moule and P. Pelliot, London, Routledge, 1938.

——*La Description du monde*, ed. L. Hambis, Paris, 1959. See also under Pelliot, P.

Pope, J. A. *Chinese Porcelain from the Ardebil Shrine*, Washington, 1956.

Reinaud, M. *Relation des voyage faits par les Arabes et les Persans dans l'Inde et en Chine*, Paris, 1845, vol. I, pp. lxi, 12 and 13.

Reusch, R. *History of East Africa*, New York, Ungar, 1961 (new edition).

Revington, T. M. "Some notes on the Mafia island group" (Mafia, Chole, Juani and Jibondo), *Tanganyika Notes and Records*, no. 10, December 1940, pp. 86 ff.

Richthofen, F. *China: Ergebnisse eigener Reisen and darauf gegründeter Studien*, 5 vols. and 2 atlases, Berlin, 1877–1912.

——*Über den Seeverkehr nach und von China im Altertum und Mittelalter*,

Verhandlungen der Berliner Gesellschaft für Erdkunde, 1876, parts 5 and 6.

Rideout, J. K. "The rise of the eunuchs during the T'ang dynasty", *Asia Major*, new series, vol. I, 1949, pp. 53–74, and vol. III, 1953, pp. 42–58.

Robinson, A. E. "Notes on saucer and bowl decorations on houses, mosques and tombs", *Tanganyika Notes and Records*, no. 10, December 1940, pp. 86 ff.

Rockhill, W. W. and Hirth, F. "Notes on the relations and trade of China with the Eastern Archipelago and the coast of the Indian Ocean during the fourteenth century", *T'oung Pao*, vol. XIV, 1913, pp. 473–6; vol. XV, 1941, pp. 419–77; vol XVI, 1915, pp. 62–159, 236–71, 374–92 and 604–26.

Schwarz, E. H. L. "The Chinese connections with Africa", *Journal of the Royal Asiatic Society of Bengal* (Calcutta), vol. IV, 1938, pp. 175–93.

Schefer, Ch. *Relations des Musulmans avec les Chinois depuis l'extension de l'Islamisme jusqu'à la fin du XV siècle*, Paris, 1895.

Schoff, W. H. *Early Communications between China and the Mediterranean*, Philadelphia, 1921.

Shinnie, P. L. "Socotra", *Antiquity*, no. 134, June 1960, pp. 100–10.

Smith, D. H. "Zaitun's five centuries of Sino-foreign trade", *Journal of the Royal Asiatic Society*, 1958, parts 3 and 4, pp. 164–77.

Stigand, C. H. *The Land of Zinj, Being an Account of British East Africa, its Ancient History and Present Inhabitants*, London, Constable, 1913.

Stowel, R. F. "Notes on some ruins at Tongoni, near Tanga", *Tanganyika Notes and Records*, no. 4, pp. 75 ff.

Strandes, J. *Die Portugiesenzeit von Deutsch- und Englisch-Ostafrika*, Berlin 1888.

——*The Portuguese Period in East Africa* (translation of the above), tr. Jean Walliwork, Nairobi, Kenya History Society, 1962.

Tanner, R. E. S. "Some Chinese pottery found at Kilwa Kisiwani", *Tanganyika Notes and Records*, no. 32, January 1952, pp. 83–4.

Teggart, F. J. *Rome and China: A Study of Correlations in Historical Events*, Berkeley, University of California Press, 1939.

T'ung Shu-yeh. "Ch'ung lun Cheng Ho hsia Hsi-yang shin-chien chih mao-i hsing-chih" (A further discussion of the commercial nature of the incident of Cheng Ho's voyages to the Western Ocean), *Yü-kung*, vol. 7, nos. 1–3, pp. 239–46.

Vel'gus, V. "O srednevekovykh kitayskikh izvestiyakh ob Afrike i nekotorykh voprosakh ikh izucheniya" (Medieval Chinese accounts of Africa and some problems of their study), *Afrikanskiy etnograficheskiy sbornik VI*, Akademiya Nauk SSSR, Moscow–Leningrad 1966, "Nauka", pp. 84–103.

——"Strany Mo-lin' i Bo-sa-lo (Lao-bo-sa) v srednevekovykh kitayskikh izvestiyakh ob Afrike" (The countries of Mo-lin and Bo-sa-lo in Chinese medieval accounts of Africa), ibid., pp. 104–21.

——"Marshrut plavaniy iz Vostochnoy Afriki v Persidskiy zaliv v VII v." (The sailing route from East Africa to the Persian Gulf in the seventh century), *Afrikanskiy etnograficheskiy sbornik VII*, Akademiya Nauk SSSR, Leningrad, "Nauka", 1969, pp. 109–26.

——"Issledovaniye nekotorykh spornykh voprosov istorii morekhodstva v Indiyskom okeane." (Some controversial questions of the history of navigation in the Indian ocean), ibid., pp. 127–76.

——"Maris (Meroe) and Beshariya in medieval Chinese sources", *Second International Congress of Africanists: Papers Presented by the USSR Delegation*, Moscow, 1967, 16 pp.

Wang Gung-wu. "The Nanhai trade: A study of the early history of Chinese trade in the South China Sea", *Journal of the Malayan Branch of the Royal Asiatic Society*, vol. XXXI, no. 182, 1958, pp. 2 ff.

Wheatley, P. "Possible references to the Malay peninsula in the Annals of the former Han", *Journal of the Malayan Branch of the Royal Asiatic Society.* vol. XXX, no. 1, 1957, pp. 115–21. On pp. 119–20 Wheatley affirms that Huang-chih was *not* in Africa, that it is unlikely that it was in the Malay peninsula, but that it is not impossible that it was a locality in Sumatra.

——"The Land of Zanj: Exegetical notes on Chinese knowledge of East Africa prior to A.D. 1500", *Geographers and the Tropics: Liverpool Essays*, London, 1964.

Worcester. *The Junks and Sampans of the Yangtze*, vol. I, 1947.

Wu Chi-hua, "Sea transportation during the Yüan and the early Ming dynasty", *Bulletin of the Institute of History and Philosophy*, vol. XXVII, 1956, pp. 363–80.

Wylie, A. "The History of the South-Western Barbarians and Chao Sëen", *Journal of the Royal Anthropological Institute*, vol. 9, 1880, p. 43.

——"Notes on the Western Regions translated from the Ts'een Han Shoo", *Journal of the Royal Anthropological Institute*, vol. 10, 1881, p. 20; vol. II, 1882, p. 83.

Yamada, Kentaro. "A Short History of Ambergris Trade by the Arabs and Chinese in the Indian Ocean", Report 8, Institute of World Economics, Kinki University, 1955.

Yamamoto, T. "Cheng Ho's expeditions to the South Sea under the Ming dynasty", *Toyo Gakuho*, vol. XXI, 1933–34, pp. 374–404 and 506–56.

Yule, Sir Henry. See under Polo, Marco.

Zimmermann, E. *Alt-chinesische Porzellane im alten Serai*, Berlin, 1930.

Index

Abdullah Ibn Yasin, 79
Abu Zayd Hasan, 41
Abul Fida, 74
Abyssinia, 5, 87
Abyssinians, 13, 77
Aden, 27, 39–40, 55, 62, 64
Africans in China, 21
Alagakkonara, King of Ceylon, 60
Alexander of Macedon, 20
Alexandria, 4, 18, 19, 20
ambergris, 24, 38, 78
America, Chinese claim to discovery of, 75
Androy, 72
Annam, 5
Arabian peninsula, 2, 18, 20, 41, 53, 72, 89
Arabs, 5, 9, 14, 19, 20, 21, 33, 45–6, 72, 74, 76
archaeology, in East Africa, 15, 41–51
archery, 23, 38, 39
A-tan (Aden), 61
Atlas, Catalan, 1
Atlas, Mongol, 25
Audemard, L., 14, 90
Azania, 24, 41, 79

Bajun islands, 3, 51, 72, 83
barter, 9–10, 15, 23
Beit al-Amani, Zanzibar, 45
Bengal, 28, 29, 30, 31
Berbera, 18–19, 20, 24, 50, 78
Bermuda rig, 11
birds, migrant, 24
Biruni, Al-, 2
Bo-ba-li, see Po-pa-li
Book of the Marvels of India, 2, 15
Brava, 37, 39, 43, 53, 55, 61, 64, 82, 83
Bretschneider, E., 50, 90
British Museum, 41, 42, 84

Buddha, 22, 63
burial customs, African, 24
burials of Chinese abroad, 17
Bushell, W. S., 42

Calicut, 13, 53, 55, 59, 61, 62, 64, 65
camels, 23, 38, 39, 61
Canton, 5, 13, 14
Cape of Good Hope, 45
celadon ware, 42, 85
Central Asia, 11, 81
Ceylon, 37, 43, 52, 53, 60, 62, 64
Chan-cheng (Chapma), 28. 59
Chang-Lo, 36, 56, 63
Chang Sheng, 52
Chang Ta, 59
Chao Ju-kua, 20, 21, 78
Chavannes, 50, 79, 90
Ch'en Tsu-yi, 64
Cheng Hao-sheng, 56
Cheng Ho, 2, 14, 28, 29, 31, 34, 35, 37, 39, 40, 41, 43, 52, 53, 54, 55, 56–65, 67, 69, 70, 72, 74, 81, 83, 86, 87, 88, 89
Cheng Tok, 85
Cheng T'ung, Emperor, 35, 71
chi deer, 38
Ch'ien-Han shu, 4
Chien-wen Ti, Emperor, 27–8, 29
ch'i-lin, see giraffe
Chin dynasty, 22
Chin Yun-ming, 56
Chittick, H. N., 50
Chou Ch'ü-fei, 22
Chou Fu, 57
Chou Shin-te, 73
Chu Liang, 57
Chu Yüan-chang, 26, 80
Ch'üan-chou (Zaytun), 8, 13, 19, 74
Chuang Wei-chi, 73

Chu-fan chih (1226), 18, 19, 21, 22
Chung-li (Somali coast), 20, 23
Chu-pu (Giumbo), 37, 38, 82
Chu Yu, 15, 73
Chwaka, 46
Ciovayi, 51
Cochin, 60, 62, 64
coin, export of Chinese, 7, 8, 9
coins, Chinese, 9, 41–3, 51
Comoro islands, 20, 36
compass, magnetic, 12, 25, 76
Cordier, H., 28, 66, 90
Coryndon Museum, Nairobi, 46
Coupland, R., 21, 90
Curle, A. T., 50, 91
customs duties, 5, 7, 14, 27

Dar es Salaam Museum, 45
Dante, *Divina Commedia*, 88
Davidson, Basil, 7, 37, 76
Duyvendak, J. J. L., 1, 14, 19, 21–5, 27, 28, 29, 30, 31, 34, 39, 52, 56–7, 73, 80, 91

East Indies, 3, 5, 20, 27, 61, 64
Egypt, 4, 14, 18, 19, 20, 70, 72, 75, 89
elephants, 88
Ethiopia, 5, 87
Ethiopians, 13, 77
eunuchs, 33, 54, 57–8, 82
Eunuchs, Department of, 4

Fa Hsien, 12, 38, 39, 54, 55, 67
Fei Hsin, 36, 81, 83
Feng-huo, naval base of, 71
Franciscan missionaries, 74
frankincense, 23, 38, 78
Freeman-Grenville, G.S.P., 42, 43, 45–6, 50, 91
Fripp, C. E., 16, 50, 91
Fu-chien, 67
Fuchs, W., 25, 92

Galla herdsmen, 19
garbassar, 39
Gedi, 46, 49
Giordano, Frate, 77
Girace, A., 37, 39, 83, 92
giraffe, 22, 23, 29, 30, 31, 40, 80

Giumbo, 37, 38, 83
Gog and Magog, 2
Great Wall of China, 26
Gujerat, 20–21

Hadramawt, 87
Hamar Gaggab, 51
Han dynasty, 4, 11, 61
Hang-chou, port of, 8, 11
Hennig, R., 5, 92
Herrmann, A., 5, 92
Hirth, F., 36, 41, 42, 50, 92
Horn of Africa, 18–19, 24, 36
Hormuz, 1, 31, 54, 59, 60, 61, 62, 64, 65, 66
Hourani, G. F., 45
Hsia Yün-chi, 67
Hsiao-ch'eng, naval base of, 71
Hsien-lo (Siam), 59
Hsin-chiang-k'ou, naval base of, 33
Hsing-ch'a sheng-lan (1436), 36, 37, 54
Hsin T'ang-shu, 19, 22, 78
Hsin-yang fan-kuo chih (1434), 82
Hsi-yang ch'ao-king tien-lu (1520), 36
Hsüan-te, Emperor, 54
Hsü-pu, naval base of, 11
hua-fu-lu (zebra), 37, 61
Huang Sheng-ts'eng, 36
Huang-chih, 5, 96
Hu-ch'a-la (Gujerat), 20–21
Hudson, G. F., 4
Hulsewé, A. F. P., 43, 45, 75
Hu-lu-mo-ssu (Hormuz), 59, 60, 61, 62, 64, 65
Hung-hsi, Emperor, 54, 67
Hung Chen, 81, 82
Hung Pao, 57
Hung-wu, Emperor, 32, 33, 34
Hunter, Graham, 46, 50
Husuni Ndogo, Kilwa, 50

Ibn Battuta, 2, 8, 13, 15, 26, 77, 86
Idrisi, Al-, 2, 24, 83
India, 5, 13, 14, 20, 21, 41, 46, 52, 53
Indians, 74
Ingrams, W. H., 41, 78
inscriptions of Cheng Ho, 31, 52–5
Inyanga, 16, 51, 72, 86
Italiaander, R., 30
ivory, 8, 21, 23, 38, 74, 78

Jackson, Sir Frederick, 45
Japan, 17, 32, 80
Japanese, 14
Java, 3, 28, 55, 59, 61, 62, 64, 65, 80
Jereza, 50
jewel ships, 34, 54, 68
Jobo, 55
Jufar, 53, 55
Jung-pang Lo, 30, 31–5, 43, 68, 70, 71, 73
junks, Chinese, 77

Kajengwa, Zanzibar, 42
Kambalu, 21
Kan-ma-li, 36
Kan-mei, 20
Kaole, 50, 84
Kao-tsung, Emperor, 7–8
Kauli, Bagamoyo, 46
Kera, 50
Kilepwa, 49
Kilifi, 49
Kilwa, 41, 44, 49, 50
King George V Memorial Museum, Nairobi, 46
Kirk, Sir John, 42
Kirkman, J., 42, 46–50, 78, 93
K'o-chih (Cochin), 59, 60, 62
Kua-wa (Java), 59, 61
Kuang-chou, 22
Kublai Khan, 81
Kukien, 28
Kulam, 38
Ku-li (Calicut), 59, 60, 61
K'un-lun (Kambalu), 21, 22
K'un-lun-ts'eng-chi islands, 20, 21
Kung Sheng, 54, 55, 67
Kuo-feng, 56
Kuwabara, J., 10, 93

La-sa (?Mombasa), 85
La-sa (?Zeila), 37, 39, 53, 55, 82
leopards, 38, 61
Liang dynasty, 40
Libya, 20
Li-ch-ien-ta (Somali coast), 36
Li Lung-mien, painter, 21
Ling-wai tai-ta (1178), 15, 22, 23
lions, 38, 40, 61, 75
Li-tai t'ung-chien chi-lan (Essentia Historiae, 18th c.), 28–9, 68

Liu-chia Chiang, 28, 36, 56, 60
Liu Chin, 82
Liu Ta-hsia, 68
Lo-p'o-ssu (Somali coast), 36
Lu Hsi-hsiang, 28
lung-chuen celadon, 45

Ma Huan, 37, 54, 67, 81
Macao, 67
Madagascar, 3, 20, 21
ma-ha animal, 37
Mafia, 41, 46
Malacca, 61, 64
Malay peninsula, 5, 20
Malay peoples, 3
Malaya, 53
Ma-lin (Malindi), 19, 29, 30, 39, 46. 49, 78, 87, 95
Man-pa-sa (Mombasa), 87
maps, Chinese, 25, 79
maps, early European, 79
Marco Polo, 8, 13, 14, 24, 26, 74, 77, 86, 94
Masai, 19
Mashonaland, 16
Mas'udi, 2
Mathew, G., 49, 50
Mau Yung-i, 57
Mauro, Fra, 2
Mecca, 27, 55
Merca, 39, 43
Migiurtinia, 24, 83
mi-li-kao animal, 61,
Ming dynasty, 1, 9, 17, 26, 27, 61, 68, 72, 82; coins of, 41–3
Ming History (*Ming shih*), 27, 39, 53, 55, 70, 78, 82
Ming-chou, port of (Ning-po), 7
Mo-ch'ieh-lao (Maghrib al-'aqsa), 19
Mogadishu, 37, 38, 39, 41, 42, 43, 51, 55, 62, 64, 83, 87
Mo Lin, see Ma-lin
Mombasa, 82, 85, 87
Mongols, 7, 26, 79
monsoon winds, 2, 7, 15, 18, 56, 66
Montecorvino, Giovanni da, 26
Mozambique, 16, 51
Mtambwe, 44
Mnara island, 49
Mu-ku-tu-shu (Mogadishu), 37, 38, 53, 61, 64, 87
Muscat, 82

Muslims, 23, 29
myrrh, 23, 38

Nan T'ang dynasty, 43
Nanking, 59, 62, 81
nautical skills, Chinese, 12–13, 35, 76
naval construction, Chinese, 7, 13, 14, 26, 28, 31–5, 67
navy, Chinese, 10–11, 15, 66–72
Ndagoni, 44
Necho, Pharaoh, 16
Needham, Joseph, 28, 76, 94
Ngomeni, 46
Ngumi, 51
Ngurumi, 50
Nicobar islands, 55

Odorico, Frate, da Pordenone, 26, 74, 86
ostriches, 22, 23, 38, 75
Ou-yang Hsiu, 19

Palembang, 53, 62
Pao Tsun-p'eng, 73
paper currency, Chinese, 9, 33, 75
Pearce, F. B., 41, 43, 50, 78
Pelliot, P., 1, 52, 53
Pemba, 20, 21, 44, 47, 78
Persian Gulf, 1, 5, 14, 18, 27, 31, 72, 82
Persians, 14, 19, 23, 25, 33, 46, 72, 74, 78
Pharos of Alexandria, 20
Phillips, M. G., 57
Phoenicians, 16, 72
P'ing-chou k'o-t'an, 15, 74
Pi-pa-lo, see Po-pa-li
Pirone, M., 37, 83
Polynesian peoples, 12, 76–7
Po-pa-li (Berbera), 18–19, 20, 22, 24, 64
p'öng birds, 21
porcelain, Chinese, 1, 8, 9, 10, 18, 43–51, 75
Portuguese, 45, 67, 72
P'o-sa, country of, 19
Ptolemy, 74
Pu-la-wa (Brava), 37, 53, 61, 87
P'u Shou-keng, 73

Ras Mkumbuu, 78
Rasini, 51
rhinoceros, 5, 38
rhinoceros horn, 8, 21, 23
Rhodesia, 16
Robinson, A. E., 50, 95
Rockhill, W. W., 2, 36, 52, 53
rudder, introduction of, 12
Rufiji river, 45

Sai-i-te Ha-san (Sayyid Hasan), 89
Sai-i-ta-li (Sayyid Ali), 70, 89
San-pao t'ai-chien hsia hsi-yang chi (1597), 88
Sayfuddin, ruler of Bengal, 29
Schwarz, E. H. L., 1, 15–17, 43, 72, 76, 95
Seng-chih, 22
she-chang (musk deer), 37
Shen Tsung, Emperor, 42
Shih-lu, 54, 88
Siam, 59, 60, 62
Si-yang fan-kou chih, 54
slaves, 7, 21–2, 25
Socotra, 24, 87
Sofala, 87
Somalis, 19, 78
Songo Mnara, 85
Strandes, J., 44
Stuhlmann, F. L., 42–4
Sui dynasty, 40
Su-kan-la (Sekander, King of Sumatra), 60
Su-lu-t'an A-shih-la-fi (Sultan of Egypt), 70
Sumatra, 3, 28, 60
Su-men-ta-la (Samudra), 60
Sung Annals, 7
Sung dynasty, 2, 7–12, 17, 26, 72; coins of, 41–3

T'ai-ts'ang chou chih, 88
T'ai-tsung, Emperor, 7
T'ang dynasty, 7, 9, 11–12, 18, 61; coins of, 41–3
T'ang kuo-shih pu, 7
Tanner, R. E. S., 44, 50, 95
Tao-i chih-lueh (1349), 36, 37, 82
Ta-shih, see Arabs
Thailand, 59, 60, 62

T'ien-fei (Celestial Spouse), 36, 56, 59, 62
T'ien-yi-ko, 39
Ting ware, 46
Ti-ping, 26, 80
Tongoni, 46
tortoise-shell, 23, 73
trade, Chinese views on, 5, 7, 8, 10, 26–7, 80
trade, expansion of Chinese, 7, 44–5, 49
tribute, to Emperor, 4, 27, 29, 31–3, 39–40, 53, 61
Tsai-nu-li-a-pi-ting (Zayn al-Abidin), 63
Ts'ong-pa (Ts'eng-pat, Ts'eng-po: Zanzibar), 18, 20, 21
Ts'eng-yao-lo, 36
tsu-la-fa (giraffe), 61
Tuan Cheng-shih, 18
T'ung-shan, naval base of, 71
Tu-shu min ch'iu chi, 82

Uganda Museum, 45
Usambara plateau, 16, 51, 72, 86

Venetians, 74
Victoria and Albert Museum, 44

Wai Sum, 75
Wang Cheng, 82
Wang Chih, 82
Wang Ching-hung, 53, 54, 57, 66
Wang Gung-wu, 73
Wang Mang, 4
Wang Po-ch'iu, 56

Wang Ta-yuan, 36
Wei Chung-hsien, 82
Wei-lio, 4, 18
Wells, H. G., 88
whales, 24
Wu, Emperor, 33
Wu Chi-hua, 73
Wu-ch'i-san, 4, 18
Wu-hsü, naval base of, 71
Wu-pei-chih map, 57
Wu-ssu-li (Misr), see Egypt

Yai-shan, battle of, 26
Yang Chen, 57
Yi-hsing, 76
ying ch'ing porcelain, 49
Ying-yai sheng-lan (c. 1425–32), 36, 37, 52, 54, 82
Youssouf Kamal, 14, 39
Yüan dynasty, 17, 26, 28, 72
Yule, Sir Henry, 13
Yung-lo, Emperor, 28–30, 33–5, 37, 72
Yu-yang tsa-tsu (ninth century), 18, 19, 22, 78

Zanzibar, 2, 18, 20, 21, 41, 42, 45, 46, 71, 78
Zayn al-Abidin, 64
Zaytun, port of (Ch'üan-chou), 8, 13, 19, 74
zebras, 22, 29, 37, 61, 75
Zeila, 37, 50, 53, 55, 82
zenj (black), 74
Zimbabwe, 43, 86
Zinj empire, 2, 9, 31, 41–51
zoo, Emperor's, in Peking, 9, 75